THE VALUE CHAIN SHIFT

Seven future challenges facing top executives

Edited by

Carlos Cordón

Teresa Ferreiro

The value chain shift: Seven future challenges facing top executives

Copyright © 2014 IMD – International Institute for Management Development
Value Chain 2020 Research Center, www.imd.org/vc2020

IMD
REAL WORLD. REAL LEARNING

Ch. de Bellerive 23, P.O. Box 915
CH-1001 Lausanne | Switzerland
Tel: +41 21 618 01 11 | Fax: +41 21 618 07 07
www.imd.org

The opinions expressed in this book are not necessarily those of the companies participating in the VC2020 project. The authors of each chapter are responsible for the content in their chapter.

Design by: Malabars – Barcelona – Spain. www.malabars.com

ISBN: 978-2-940485-08-6

Table of contents

Chapter 1   27

Measuring corporations' cost and contribution to society

Polina Bochukova, Carlos Cordón, Teresa Ferreiro

Chapter 2   43

Managing resource scarcities

Arjan van Weele, Luis Vivanco

Chapter 3   59

Scale and speed: Traditional multinationals versus emerging market firms

Howard Yu, Teresa Ferreiro

List of figures

List of tables

Contributors

Alexander Arsath	Former VC2020 core team member, former program manager, NEVI, the Netherlands
Polina Bochukova	VC2020 core team member, associated researcher, IMD, Switzerland
Carlos Braga	Professor of Internal Political Economy, IMD, Switzerland
Bettina Büchel	VC2020 Theme 4 co-leader, Professor of Strategy and Organization, IMD, Switzerland
Salvatore Cantale	Professor of Finance, IMD, Switzerland
Carlos Cordón	VC2020 director and core team member, VC 2020 Theme 1 and Theme 6 leader, Professor of Supply Chain Management (LEGO Chair), IMD, Switzerland
Wouter Crul	Former VC2020 core team member, former managing director at NEVI-Purspective, The Netherlands
Nuno Fernandes	Professor of Finance, IMD, Switzerland
Teresa Ferreiro	VC2020 relationship manager and core team member, associated researcher, IMD, Switzerland
Mark Foster	VC2020 core team member, chairman of the International Business Leaders Forum (IBLF), executive in residence at IMD, Switzerland
James Henderson	Professor of Strategic Management, IMD, Switzerland
Irene Kamp	Former VC2020 core team member, former research associate, NEVI, the Netherlands
Jean-Pierre Lehmann	Professor of Internal Political Economy, IMD, Switzerland
Thomas Malnight	Professor of Strategy and General Management, IMD, Switzerland

Daina Mazutis	Professor of Strategy, Leadership and Ethics, IMD, Switzerland
Winter Nie	Professor of Operations and Service Management, IMD, Switzerland
Ralf Seifert	Professor of Operations Management, IMD, Switzerland
Francisco Szekely	Professor of Global Leadership and Sustainability, IMD, Switzerland
Luis Vivanco	VC2020 team member, associated researcher, IMD, Switzerland
Michael Wade	VC2020 Theme 4 co-leader, Professor of Innovation and Strategic Information Management, IMD, Switzerland
Arjan van Weele	VC2020 core team member, VC2020 Theme 2 and Theme 7 leader, Professor of Purchasing and Supply Management (NEVI chair), Eindhoven University of Technology, the Netherlands
Howard Yu	VC2020 Theme 3 leader, Professor of Strategic Management and Innovation, IMD, Switzerland
E. Zappone-Fabre	VC2020 Theme 5 leading expert, partner at Dyator, Switzerland
Christopher Zintel	Research associate, IMD, Switzerland

Our very special thanks to the following people and those who enriched the VC2020 project, the research and the two-year journey:

- Anne-Séverine Vinet, IMD Global Value Chain Center (VC2020) coordinator, who made everything run smoothly and efficiently.
- The generosity and openness of the VC2020 participating companies and especially the representatives of each for their active participation in the forums, work streams and different activities over these two years.
- The institutions, experts and top executives beyond the VC2020 core group who collaborated on the research, workshops, activities and discovery trips and helped the project progress.

Foreword

We live in volatile times. The certainties of steady global growth that characterized the last decade do not exist in this one. As business leaders work hard to move their organisations forward in an era of slower growth and mixed economic indicators, the strategies and skills necessary to succeed are broader and more nuanced than before.

IMD's VC2020 project has recognized this reality and sought to give these leaders some signposts that will point the way as we head towards 2020. As the research has shown, for all the volatility, there are some things we can be sure about: the evolution of a more multipolar global economy, with new centres of economic activity, will continue as we see the rapid maturing of emerging markets; the explosion in the pervasiveness of technology and its application to all aspects of life will only expand; and the issues of natural resource access and security will come ever more to the fore in the context of an increasing world population that seeks to consume ever more of the earth resources.

The value chains of all organizations will need to reflect and respond to these realities as the strategies, operating models, processes and systems are adapted to provide both certainty and adaptability in a fast-moving environment of shifting demands. This research project has engaged a unique range of business, academic and other stakeholder groups to try to envisage the extrapolation of these and other trends and draw out the critical "so what" for business and supply chain leadership.

What have we learnt? We have seen that the very basis of business success and its measurement will come under pressure to change as the licence to operate for business within society comes into question. As we imagine the various scenarios for the future relationship between business and its wider societal stakeholders, they all point to a vastly enhanced awareness in business of the nature of the contract that it has to serve its customers, support the needs of citizens and play a part in the development of thriving and sustainable societies. This has big implications for leaders in the way that they connect with, and are aware of, the wider world in which they work.

Resource scarcity will be one of the drivers for these new relationships, as it becomes a strategic issue for all businesses. There are pessimists who believe that the world is going to "hell in a handcart" and that the growing demands on finite sources will end in tears, and optimists who believe that technology and human ingenuity will come to the rescue of us all. The research has validated that both views are partly right but also reinforced that, whatever your position as a company, you need to have an active strategy with regard to resource management to take control of your destiny. The links to the role within society and its expectations are also evident.

New entrants from the multipolar world are creating challenges for traditional multinationals by taking advantage of new paradigms of speed, cost and flexibility they have developed in serving their initial domestic markets. These new competitors have the advantage of playing on home turf in the fastest growing parts of the world and they have the street smarts that come from winning at the bottom of the pyramid. The research has reinforced the strengths that make these players effective on the wider world stage and stressed the need for Western companies to engage deeply and proactively in seeking their own growth, on their own terms, in the rising markets of the east and south.

In a fast-changing world, with rapid information flows and the emergence of new customers and business partners, it is not surprising that speed has been a key topic of discussion in the group. Not speed in isolation, but in conjunction with that other balancing factor of risk. The work has drawn upon a number of examples in different industries and brought out the relationship between the demands of customer value, the resources an organization can access, its partners and its processes to create the concept of "optimal speed". It is clear that the context in which the company works and the nature of its business cycles do influence both the natural "clock speed" and the scale of the bets it is able to make. Creating an explicit awareness of this is a path to competitive advantage, particularly when it can shape your fundamental market position with the customers you seek and the responsiveness they demand.

The concept of the ecosystem has been the buzzword of organization strategy for a while now and this research has validated that, if anything, the requirement for businesses to shape their external features as much as their internal models will be even more critical. Everything points to valuing and reinforcing the connections with partners at least as much as the internal management nodes. This has huge implication for the leaders too and, taken together with the wider societal role I have mentioned, requires them to be broader, more outward-looking and able to interact as well with their peers as they do with their subordinates.

In today's world the underpinning of the organization by enterprise systems and wider IT is a given. The power of technology to increase connectivity with customers, enable speed and flexibility, as well as harness the impact of the ecosystem is going to be more and more important. The team identified the key success factors to supporting local market needs in the context of fine-tuned global processes. By exercising judgment with regard to engagement, leadership and governance, and having the sophistication and thoughtfulness of approach to draw the right line on the degree of mandated standardization, better, more fit-for-purpose solutions are possible in the field, which is otherwise awash with failed projects.

The thread that has run through this work is the externalization of the modern business and the very deep way in which a successful organization and its value chain need to look beyond the four walls of the enterprise. Whether it is connecting via social media with customers, building strategic relationships with ecosystem partners or learning how to succeed in emerging markets, the winning VC2020 player is super-aware of the wider environment in which it operates. It is no surprise then to see the theme of corporate social responsibility (CSR) also evolving from the traditional world of corporate philanthropy, image enhancement and employee engagement (all of which remain important of course) to a more strategic underpinning of the enterprise. Our businesses will succeed when they most help the societies that they work in to thrive and grow. Organisations will need to build trust to form lasting relationships with the populations they serve and the regulatory environments in which they find themselves – a new shared value chain 2020!

I think that the teams involved in this work have produced some important new insights into the way we will all be working in the years to come and I hope that you will enjoy reading the practical ideas, frameworks and approaches drawn from current business examples and real-life experiences of business leaders, which this book contains. The coming decade will indeed hold many uncertainties and the path will not always be clear but the pointers provided by VC2020 will, I believe, help to show the way.

Mark Foster

Chairman, International Business Leaders Forum (IBLF)

Introduction

Carlos Cordón

Introduction

Carlos Cordon

At the end of 2011, executives who are responsible for the value chains[1] of 10 multinational companies discussed and agreed on the research questions (themes) that will address the most important challenges they will face in the year 2020. They settled on seven research questions, which correspond to the chapters of this book. Each question resulted in a work stream, with its own team led by an IMD professor and including representatives from the companies, plus a number of researchers and experts.

These questions are very broad, and it might be surprising that they come from executives responsible for supply chains. We believe that this is the consequence of a big shift; value chains are central to a company's existence, they revolutionize the way we see the economy and they are a main driver of the world, as we know it today.

Together with these executives, we explored the research questions with the objective of providing useful insights for companies. This collaborative journey has produced several papers, workshops, discovery trips, presentations, working tools, webcasts and, finally, this book. The primary objective of the research was to find better answers from a company executive's point of view, rather than from an academic point of view. Over the two-year course of our research, we discovered unexpected findings that have made the journey much more valuable than we expected.

---

1. This book uses a broad definition of the terms "value chain" and "supply chain" in which both are interchangeable and include all players in the chain from the upstream suppliers to the downstream end consumer.

The very broad responsibilities of supply chain executives

After a quick read of the following research questions, the first thing that comes to mind is that they are broad:

1. What is a company's cost and contribution to society?
2. How can resource scarcity be managed?
3. How are companies from emerging countries managing their value chains?
4. Which processes should IT manage globally and which ones should it manage locally?
5. What kind of leadership will be required in future value chains?
6. How are speed, risk, opportunity and business models related in value chains?
7. How is corporate social responsibility evolving in value chains?

Some people were of the opinion that the first question is a philosophical one. It requires defining what is good and bad. The real issue is, as a top supply chain executive put it, "I am responsible for anything that could go wrong." That means that supply chains might often be companies' biggest cost to society. If we look at the impact of big companies' decisions on their suppliers, and their suppliers' suppliers, it is easy to see how big corporations impact millions of people lives and the environment.

The crisis of 2008 revealed that the idea that governments should leave business alone, as this was the most efficient way of running the economy, was totally inadequate. At that time, governments all over the world saved car companies, banks and others, using public money to fix what companies had broken. Consequently, society and government are duty-bound to ask companies how they are contributing to the society that saved them. Companies must not be left alone, as 2008 proved.

But why bother about the contribution corporations make? Given that companies are a cost to society, the question of what they are contributing becomes fundamental to justifying why they have the right to exist. The research issue is how to measure the contribution, i.e. how to develop a good measurement tool that executives can use. Given that value chains tends to be one of the biggest cost and value components of an organization, this question becomes fundamental when evaluating supply chain decisions in companies.

At the same time, economists' views of the world economy are undergoing a huge shift because of global value chains. The majority of economic models assume that countries make finished products and that all of the product's value is added in a country. For example, those models assume that if the Apple iPhone is made in China 100% of its value is added in China. It turns out that less than 5% of an iPhone's value is added in China, making the previous assumption an overestimation by a factor of 20. Therefore, many economic models about growth, labor and competition between countries might be fundamentally wrong. In the book *Outsourcing Economics: Global Value Chains in Capitalist Development*,[2] Milberg and Winkler argue that most economic models and the government policies derived from them should be rebuilt from scratch taking into account the reality of global value chains.

The impact of value chains and outsourcing is so big that the World Trade Organization (WTO) is fundamentally changing the way the economy is measured. Currently, the key measure has been gross domestic product (GDP), measured as the value of products and services made in a country. As the iPhone example shows, GDP can overstate the value added. In the future, the WTO is going to measure value added, i.e. how much value is added in a country. Considering more than 50% of world trade consists of semi-finished products or activities that are part of the final product or service, this change to make the measure more reliable is greatly overdue.

Thus, the evolution of global value chains is fundamentally affecting the way the world economy works, and it is creating a huge challenge for economists and politicians in their quest to understand how it works. Logically, the decisions executives make about their value chains has and will impact the way the world economy works.

As a consequence, executives must consider the impact of their value-chain decisions on society. This is the main objective of the first question. However,

---

2. Milberg, William and Deborah Winkler. Outsourcing Economics: Global Value Chains in Capitalist Development. Cambridge: Cambridge University Press, 2013.

the question is very broad and the impact of the value-chain decisions made by executives is very context dependent. For this reason, we developed four scenarios under the Theme 1 framework. The measures and the appropriate decision-making tools depend very much on the scenario in which those decisions are made.

The need to understand the holistic view of the value chain

Every decision made in the supply chain has many consequences, so each decision should be an integral part of the overall management of the supply chain, dispelling the notion that supply chain managers should have expertise in one field.

Supply chain managers who do not have a broader view are prone to missing important developments that will have implications for their value chains. Take copper, for example. The threat of a copper shortage has been a supply chain issue for decades. However, innovation over the years and the discovery of new deposits kept reserves steady at around 30 more years of consumption for the last two decades, and in more recent times, it has increased to 40 years. Thus, one can conclude that what was believed to be a scarcity of copper was, in fact, just volatility. Yet supply chain managers who were focused on copper missed a more worrying scarcity – water. Thanks to the Energy Security and Water Resources Section of the United Nations,[3] it has become obvious to the world that there is a huge challenge with respect to the availability of fresh water. Water, food and energy availability are very much related because fresh water is required to produce food and energy. We have extended this into a model that includes industrial materials and infrastructure (refer to *Figure 1*).

Although this model has not yet been tested econometrically, it makes sense. The availability of food, energy and industrial materials is heavily impacted by the availability of fresh water. Similarly, the availability of fresh water, energy, food and industrial materials is impacted by the infrastructure that allows them to be efficiently transported.

---

3. For more information, visit the following website: www.unescap.org/esd/Energy-Security-and-Water-Resources/

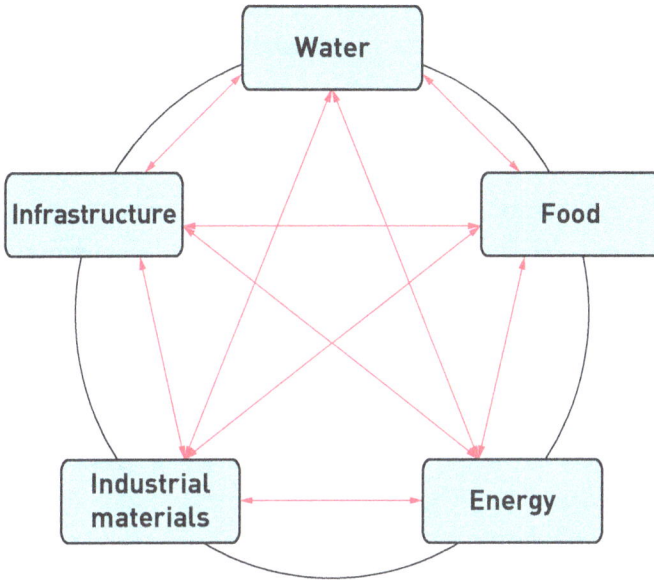

Figure 1: Interaction between resources[4]

The immediate consequence is that decisions cannot be made in isolation. For example, the idea of having purchasing managers specialized in certain commodities while ignoring the rest of the elements in *Figure 1* is becoming obsolete. Similarly, making decisions about supply chains without considering all of the elements in *Figure 1* would not make sense. The reality is that many executives intuitively consider those elements; our argument is that it should be done in a systematic and consistent way.

Our research also uncovered a somewhat discouraging fact. Many companies are investing a lot of resources in CSR, but these efforts are not providing much value. CSR has become very publicized and many non-governmental organizations (NGOs) use it as a tool to promote their own points of view and interests. As a result, companies have been forced by society and other external players to increase their CSR measures and report on how they are affecting society and the environment. The outcome has been that companies have undertaken a huge number of measures, resulting in CSR reports growing to the point where they are bigger than the companies' annual reports. Consequently,

---

4. Source: VC2020 research.

it could be argued that the CSR reports are losing their value. Still, companies must produce them to avoid being accused of not being transparent.

Coming changes to the supply chain

Several research questions were aimed at trying to understand how the supply chain is going to evolve in the future. We looked at emerging markets, the dilemma of going global while maintaining local flexibility and the leaders of those future supply chains.

Companies in emerging countries are experts in supply chains in other new countries and they are going to exploit that advantage. As we researched how companies use their supply chains to compete in emerging countries, we realized that they are much faster, more entrepreneurial and take more risks. We also realized that those companies are not looking at "developed markets" as their main targets; instead, they are focusing on other emerging markets because they know them better and there are many more opportunities. The competitive landscape is shifting to new markets, not old ones. And these competitors have bigger ambitions, e.g. "How can we multiply our business by 10 in 10 years."

When dealing with global supply chains, many global companies have standardized their processes and supporting IT systems. Through the research, detailed in Chapter 4, it has become evident that the path towards globalizing processes is paved with challenges of rigidity and almost chaos. A few companies have reached the holy grail of global standards and local flexibility and all of them have gone through a painful journey. The question today is what should be considered core and, therefore, standard all over the world and what should be adapted to local conditions. The key for executives is to manage the boundaries between the core and the edge.

We also looked at the leadership challenges supply chain leaders will face in the future. It became evident that companies are still struggling with defining the particular competencies and skills that those leaders should have because, compared with finance or marketing, there is not much of a track record of what is required for success. Simultaneously, the future will require skills that are much more related to a holistic understanding of the business and the leadership transitions necessary to lead supply chains. The conclusion is that rather than the old perception of highly specialized and technically savvy executives, the future is about managing relations across an ecosystem and understanding how to create value by joining the resources of different companies.

Finally, we looked at the relation between speed, risk, opportunities and business models. It became evident that while the motto over the last decades has been "the faster the better," the reality is that businesses are not always doing things faster for very good reasons. There is a kind of optimal speed for every supply chain and every context. Over the years, organizations have reached that optimal speed and it is ingrained in their processes and business models. The challenge is that speed depends very much on the context. In emerging markets, most companies require greater speed because of the size of the opportunities. In mature markets, changes in the environment are requiring some companies to accelerate their "cruise speed." As a consequence, many traditional organizations require a business model transformation to compete in new markets and, sometimes, to be able to compete in markets where the context has changed.

The methodology

A team of 25 experts and researchers, including 14 IMD professors, worked on this research project. The core team was composed of eight people with different backgrounds and expertise.

The research was broken down into seven questions. One group was created to work on each question, and at least one IMD professor led each group. The participating companies joined two or three of these groups, where they played an active role participating in interviews, meetings, sharing information, providing the best inside expertise depending on the research topic and opening the door for access to confidential information. It was a groundbreaking way of working, a journey of joint learning and joint development of the tools that helped us find answers to the seven questions.

Communication and interchange were key to achieving results. Three two-day forum meetings per year were held at IMD to discuss and share the state of the art and the latest findings. The research encouraged collaboration, with participants exchanging roles and presenting the outcome of their work rather than just listening. Furthermore, regular workshops, meetings, calls or internal discussions were organized for each of the seven themes.

Each theme set up its own research agenda, "feuille de route" and objectives. A detailed project plan with timelines, deliverables and goals was elaborated and shared with the core team. Webcasts, newsletters and a regularly updated website also ensured that the research reached all the parties involved.

Besides the independent research of the different teams, the VC2020 core team kept on with its regular communications and internal meetings. One of the key aspects of these sessions was to share the evolution and learning of each of the research themes, which facilitated synergies. It also helped us verify that similar concerns, approached from different perspectives by the different research teams, reached similar conclusions.

In addition to this book, the deliverables of the VC2020 project, which included case studies, papers, publications, slide presentations and videos, will be kept confidential and available only to the VC2020 sponsoring companies.

Conclusion

Two years ago, we embarked on this journey to determine what trends and new practices supply chain executives would be facing in 2020. It has been a collaborative effort in which the executives of the participating companies have been the driving force guiding our research.

We discovered much more than we expected; global supply chains are fundamentally redesigning the world economy and its well-being. The challenges ahead for those managing them are new and exciting. Supply chain leaders will have to become orchestrators who consider the implications of their decisions for the world.

The future

This two-year journey has been the beginning of on-going research that will continue in 2014. Some of the initial questions resulted in new questions for which we will try to find answers during the coming year. For example:

- Are the measurements we are proposing to evaluate the cost and contribution of a company to society realistic? A good way to find out is to test them with a real business.

- How will social media affect the value chain's processes and functioning? How should the large amount of data coming from the web be handled?

- Are companies able to track their suppliers and expect them to deliver the standards of quality that society is demanding?

Chapter 1
Measuring corporations' cost and contribution to society

Polina Bochukova
Carlos Cordón
Teresa Ferreiro

Chapter 1
Measuring corporations' cost and contribution to society[5]

Polina Bochukova
Carlos Cordón
Teresa Ferreiro

Executive summary

Prior to the 2008 crisis, it was an (almost) universally held belief that business should be conducted for the benefit of shareholders. Governments should interfere as little as possible with business to avoid hampering efficiency, wealth creation and economic growth. That world collapsed in 2008. During the months following the Lehman Brothers debacle, politicians and governments across the globe were forced to save their countries' largest businesses, from auto manufacturing to banking. This soon became a tragi-comedy. The CEOs of America's largest automotive companies flew to Washington in their luxurious private jets asking for bailouts worth billions in taxpayer money. Since then, it has become more openly recognized that businesses depend on a variety of different stakeholders and today's business leaders increasingly need to show how they create value for stakeholders along the entire value chain of their products or services.

While there is a proliferation of "social responsibility reports" that aim to show how businesses create value for society, we still lack a commonly accepted framework for measuring and comparing this type of value. To help fill this gap, we developed four different scenarios that describe how corporations' cost and contribution to society might be measured in the year 2030. Based on the insights from these scenarios, we designed a framework for measuring

5. We thank all who participated in the interviews and workshop for their insights, which greatly assisted our research.

the value and cost of businesses to society. Finally, we developed a high-level example of how this framework could be applied in practice.

Measuring corporations' cost and contribution to society: The times they are a-changin'[6]

Ask mid-level managers in any business what they see as their company's contribution to society and you are bound to receive a huge variety of answers. Just a quick sampling of responses might include the total sum of employee salaries, new products launched which make customers' lives easier or more fun, taxes paid last year, philanthropic giving, pro-bono activities in disadvantaged communities, etc. The list could easily go on, – the same question posed a decade ago would have produced the mainstream assumption mentioned above: shareholder value, also known as higher profits, rising stock prices, creating wealth for the company's owners.

Indeed, after 2008 the public discourse around the role of corporations in society has shifted from a narrow focus on shareholder value creation to a need to fulfill broader responsibilities. Investors, regulators and NGOs are holding businesses to higher standards and today's business leaders need to show how they create value for stakeholders along the entire value chain of their products or services, not just for their shareholders. This has spun off rich theoretical debates on how to reform capitalism and improve management practice. There have been calls for ethical capitalism, responsible, compassionate capitalism as well as green, sustainable, strategic and customer-driven capitalism. We have witnessed the rise of state capitalism in emerging markets and lemon socialism[7] in developed economies.

Business leaders have responded enthusiastically. According to a recent study, 93% of CEOs believe sustainability will be critical to the future success of their firm and that, moving forward, it will be important to embed the concept into

---

6. Bob Dylan. "The Times They are a-Changin'." Song from the album *The Times They are a-Changin'*, 1964.

7. Lemon socialism is when taxpayers bear the cost if things go wrong while stockholders and executives get the benefits if things go right. Krugman, Paul. "Bailouts for Bunglers." *The New York Times*, February 1, 2009.

how employees and executives think about strategy and execution.[8] Company performance along environmental and social parameters is also increasingly being tracked resulting in ever more elaborate CSR reports. Strategic theorizing has followed suit with shared value capturing the hearts and minds of boards around the globe. Older theories such as managing for stakeholders have found renewed interest by practitioners.

Houston, we have a problem: The inadequacy of available measures

However, for all the hype and excitement about driving change, doing "good" and providing a meaningful contribution to solving humanity's problems, business leaders still face a major roadblock – the problem of measurement.

As we know, managers tend to focus attention on things that lead to higher performance based on what actually gets measured. When it comes to sustainability performance, creating social value or avoiding costs for society and the planet – we are drowning in measures. Compounding the problem of abundance is the fact that the definitions of these measures are often open to interpretation, which has made performance tracking over time or between companies very difficult. From the point of view of the general public, it is basically impossible to judge if the performance communicated in company sustainability reports is good or bad, how it compares with what other companies are achieving and whether the goals pursued are transformational, aspirational or mediocre.

Let us take an example. Stora Enso Oyj purportedly descends from the world's oldest corporation, a vast copper mine in Sweden called Stora Kopparberg[9] established in the 13th century with a royal charter.[10] Today Stora Enso is a somewhat typical Scandinavian conglomerate with 28,000 employees and a global footprint spanning more than 35 countries. Its purpose is to "Do good for the people and the planet" and its *Global Responsibility Report 2012* is 72 pages long packed with metrics and measures of how the company achieves

---

8. UN Global Compact and Accenture 2010 quoted in: Maltz, E., and S. Schein. "Cultivating shared value initiatives: A three Cs approach." *Journal of Corporate Citizenship*, Iss. 47, 2012: 55–74.

9. Rothkopf, David. *Power Inc: The Epic Rivalry Between Big Business and Government and the Reckoning That Lies Ahead.* New York: Farrar, Straus and Giroux, 2012.

10. Lindroth, S. *Mining and Copper Metallurgy in Stora Kopparberg until the Beginning of the Nineteenth Century.* Upsala: Almqvist and Wiksell, 1955 (in Swedish).

that mission in practical terms. Except that there is nothing practical about these measures as they run into the hundreds and for a lay observer it is basically impossible to understand to what extent the company manages to fulfill its mission of doing good. Stora Enso is hardly a case in isolation.

Compare this with the measures used in a shareholder-centric world. Financial return, whether expressed as profit, return on investment (ROI), economic rent or shareholder return, is an elegant measure. It is simple and comparable across companies and sectors. Most of the time it is reliable (bar the odd Enron or WorldCom fiasco). Going back to our earlier example, Stora Enso's website shows just four financial targets and even if one is completely unfamiliar with the terminology,[11] it is fairly easy to see if the company has achieved its goals or not.

That corporations' primary responsibility is to maximize shareholder value was a well-known fact to business schools, corporate lawyers, judges, shareholders and not least, the C-suite (it still is in some circles and certainly in most mainstream MBA curricula). In fact, two centuries of economics and finance theorizing almost convinced us that "social welfare is maximized when all firms in an economy maximize total firm value."[12] While this assertion is not entirely untrue, it is a half-truth. What the statement (un)helpfully omits is that there should be no monopolies or externalities.[13] As long as either monopolies or externalities exist, maximizing the value for shareholders of individual firms does not maximize social welfare. Widespread pollution, the depletion of shared resources and climate change – all examples of externalities – have become a fact of modern day life. In a world like this, maximizing shareholder value does not maximize social outcomes. To sum up, while shareholder value was a perfect measure in a system geared towards maximizing the interests of shareholders, it is inadequate in a world that cares for the interests of all stakeholders, not just shareholders.

---

11. Operational ROCE (%), debt/equity ratio, dividend and distribution/share, payout ratio (%) are the four financial metrics tracked by the descendant of the world's oldest corporation.

12. Jensen, M. "Value maximization, stakeholder theory, and the corporate objective function." *Business Ethics Quarterly*, Vol. 12, Iss. 2, 2002: 235–256.

13. Externalities are situations in which the decision maker does not bear the full cost or benefit consequences of his or her choices. Water and air pollution are classic examples.

The importance of the goal and the context

This leads us to an important consideration – measuring the corporations' cost and contribution to society is goal and context dependent. For example, countries measure GDP because it is believed that higher GDP means economic development and social development. Thus, GDP helps us understand if the actions of a country are helping its development. The goal is to become a developed country. Back to the issue of considering all the stakeholders of a corporation, we should define the goal and the context to define the appropriate measures. To do so, we have developed a series of scenarios, each having a different context for the measures. If we select one scenario as our goal, we could propose the measures that we believe could lead to such a scenario.

Using a scenario-planning methodology, we identified 10 key uncertainties that might impact the way companies' cost and contribution to society are measured in the year 2030 and grouped these into five categories: consumers and society, technology, economy and investors, governance and regulation. For example, one of the key uncertainties is related to the prevalence of socially responsible consumption in the future. Socially conscious consumers "take into account the public consequences of [their] private consumption or attempt to use [their] purchasing power to bring about social change."[14] A society where consumers are predominantly socially responsible would give higher rewards to companies that appear socially responsible in comparison with those that appear less socially responsible. This in turn could have an impact on companies' top lines and would produce a different value measurement in economic terms.

Four scenarios for the year 2030

So how will the world look in the distant 2030? Will it be a world in which society plays a predominant role and decision making is collaborative? Or will it be a world with no social cohesion? Will investors commit to a sustainable future by taking long-term decisions? Will they opt for short-term gains? Or will their role be insignificant?

---

14. Webster, Jr., F.E. "Determining the characteristics of the socially conscious consumer." *Journal of Consumer Research*, Vol. 2, December, 1975: 188–196.

We developed four different scenarios to try to imagine how value might be perceived and measured in the future. We used four criteria in developing these scenarios:

- *Relevant.* The context or worlds depicted are useful in thinking about the central question.

- *Plausible.* The context or worlds depicted are believable.

- *Divergent.* The context or worlds depicted are interestingly very different in relation to the central question.

- *Challenging.* The context or worlds depicted challenge mainstream assumptions about how companies' cost and contribution to society will be valued in the future.

The scenarios are called *States and resource dilemmas, High-speed capitalism, Happy flower* and *Constructive collaboration* and (see **Figure 1.1** for a schematic representation of these contexts).

States and resource dilemmas. Set against a backdrop of high income inequality and scarce resources, state capitalism is the predominant economic model as political leaders strengthen their hold on the economy to try to manage the threat of significant social unrest. Multinational companies have some of their assets nationalized as governments struggle to feed their populations. In some countries, barter has returned as a means of exchanging essential goods. Regional conflicts are on the rise.

High-speed capitalism. New sources of energy are fueling a tide of economic growth which has lifted most boats, albeit some more than others. Investors pursue short-term strategies – so short, in fact, that the average stock in 2030 is held for no more than 4.3 seconds, according to statistics published by the World Federation of Stock Exchanges in November 2030. The geo-economic landscape is defined by the pious following of the free-market doctrine around the globe, with fewer and fewer outposts of divergence left. Consumers are

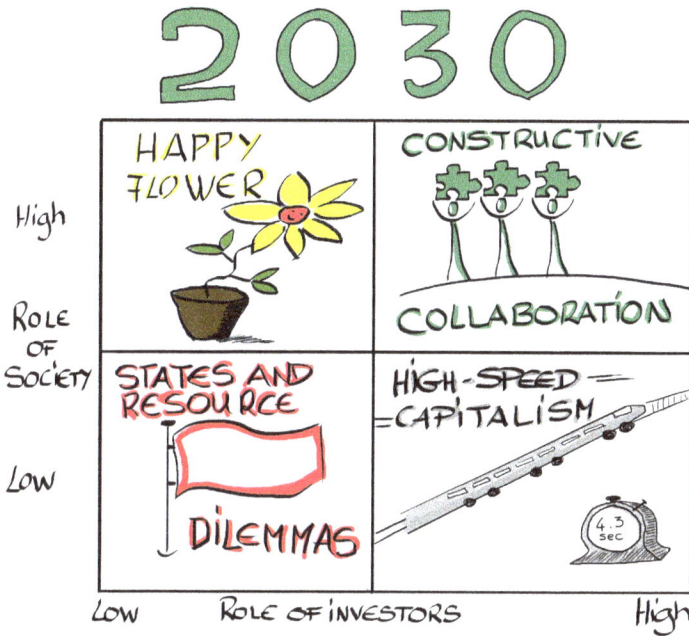

Figure 1.1: **Schematic representation of the four scenarios**[15]

largely indifferent to the political process. Governments have given up their major regulatory aspirations, seemingly for good.

Happy flower. People are increasingly losing their trust in corporations amid the rise of major climate-related catastrophes and scientific discoveries about the harmful effects of genetically modified organisms and industrial chemicals commonly used in production. The food industry is haunted by the effects of the growing social stigma of consuming processed food high in fat, sugar and salt. People are demanding new legislation that makes companies bear all the social and environmental costs of operating. Social media and other new technologies make it possible to organize individuals on a large scale, and this becomes a major driving force for change around the globe.

Constructive collaboration. A world with a growing number of economic centers of activity. Yesterday's emerging economies have become today's leaders, or powers with significant geopolitical and geo-economic clout. Data transparency

15. Source: VC2020 research. Designed by Sylvia Ischer.

is pervasive, with information ranging from product ingredients to social trivia to government decision-making processes available at the click of a button. Investors have long-term investment horizons and duly include environmental, governance and social risks in their valuations. Socially responsible investments have experienced phenomenal growth rates and represent 50% of total financial flows internationally, up from a paltry 11% in 2013.[16]

Scenario observations

States and resource dilemmas. State-owned enterprises (SOEs) become the dominant productive force in society. SOEs have always been an important element of most economies, including the most advanced ones. A recent investigation of the world's 2,000 largest companies, the so-called Forbes Global 2000, revealed that more than 10% of these firms were majority state-owned. The aggregate sales of these large, blue chip SOEs were equivalent to 6% of the world's gross national income (GNI).[17] What this scenario would mean for measuring corporations' cost and contribution to society would largely depend on state objectives. In most countries, the government explicitly aims to improve the quality of environmental and social conditions.[18] Other important objectives might include employment, growth, equity, regional development, education, health and social care.[19] Following this line of argument, we can foresee that corporations would be expected to fulfill the criteria set by the state. They should be able to demonstrate convincingly how they contribute to regional development or educational goals, for example. In this sense, states and resource dilemmas would necessitate a significant departure from the shareholder value doctrine.

High-speed capitalism. This is perhaps the simplest from a measurement point of view, as the doctrine of shareholder value maximization would

16. Data for the US market. US SIF (The Forum for Sustainable and Responsible Investment) website.

17. Including domestic and foreign subsidiaries of these companies; Kowalski, P. *et al.* "State-owned enterprises: Trade effects and policy implications." *OECD Trade Policy Paper*, No. 147, OECD Publishing, 2013.

18. OECD 2010. *Taxation, innovation and the environment.* Paris: OECD quoted in: Lammertjan, D. and B. Scholtens. "Does ownership type matter for corporate social responsibility?" *Corporate Governance: An International Review*, Vol. 20, Iss. 3, 2012: 233–252.

19. Lammertjan, D. and B. Scholtens. "Does ownership type matter for corporate social responsibility?" *Corporate Governance: An International Review*, Vol. 20, Iss. 3, 2012: 233–252.

continue to dominate. Because of the high transaction costs associated with public listing, a possible outcome might be that more and more companies go private. Alternatively, ownership might become even more fragmented than today, if crowd financing becomes a credible source of capital. In either case, the composition of shareholders might differ from today, but this would not imply a need for different measures of the corporations' cost and contribution to society.

Happy flower. Similarly, a happy flower scenario would call for different measures. If anything, a sign of shareholder value would be considered a disadvantage in this scenario and companies might look for ways to downplay its magnitude and emphasize the value they create for consumers, society and environmental preservation.

Constructive collaboration. This is the most challenging scenario from the vantage point of measuring the corporations' cost and contribution to society. It is characterized by the proactive and positive collaboration of many stakeholders, which implies that the value and the cost should be measured by taking into account all of those stakeholders. Because of its collaborative nature and high level of transparency, this scenario would necessitate almost full visibility and documentation of the results of corporate activities.

As stated before, both the goal and the context are important to elaborate the appropriate measures. The scenarios provide the context. The goal of the Value Chain 2020 project is to move the world towards the constructive collaboration scenario. The measures should be meaningful and they should drive decisions toward the ideal scenario of constructive collaboration.

Proposed framework for measuring corporations' cost and contribution to society

Building on the scenarios and prior methodologies for measuring corporations' cost and contribution to society, we propose a new framework, which is presented in ***Figure 1.2***. The full list of stakeholders that corporations interact with and cater to is outlined on the vertical axis. The summary of all categories on the vertical should add up to "society." The item "society at large" in essence denotes the groups that have not been captured under any of the other headings. On the horizontal, we divide the corporations' assets and liabilities under three headings: economic, social and environmental. The framework will use multiple currencies and will contain several indicators within each cross section of the vertical and horizontal.

Our proposal is based on several core principles briefly described below:

- *Leverage available data and concepts.* Corporations already collect and report a vast array of metrics relating to their cost and contribution to society. Some frameworks have a specific focus on environmental reporting, such as the EU Eco-Management and Audit Scheme (EMAS); others are broader and include additional aspects of performance. For example, the Balanced Scorecard measures firm performance from the perspective of finance, customers, innovation and learning and internal efficiency. The Triple Bottom Line, another framework, is based on the idea that businesses create economic, environmental and social value or costs. These and other efforts have been consolidated in the Global Reporting Initiative (GRI). Our framework will use the indicators specified by GRI as a starting point. In addition, the methodology uses the Triple Bottom Line terminology of economic, environmental and social value added.

- *Balance sheet approach.* We favor a balance sheet approach vs. an income statement approach for the purposes of this methodology. To clarify, the balance sheet approach in financial accounting terms, views the accurate determination of assets and liabilities as the primary goal of financial reporting with earnings determined as the change in net assets over a *given* time period. The income statement approach, in contrast, views the determination of earnings as primary with balance sheet items determined residually. In essence, we believe that the proposed framework has to measure the corporations' standing in society at any given point in time rather than to express the cost and contribution to society over a given time period. Why is that important? Taking a balance sheet approach will solve the potential problem of short-termism. Since we propose to use multiple

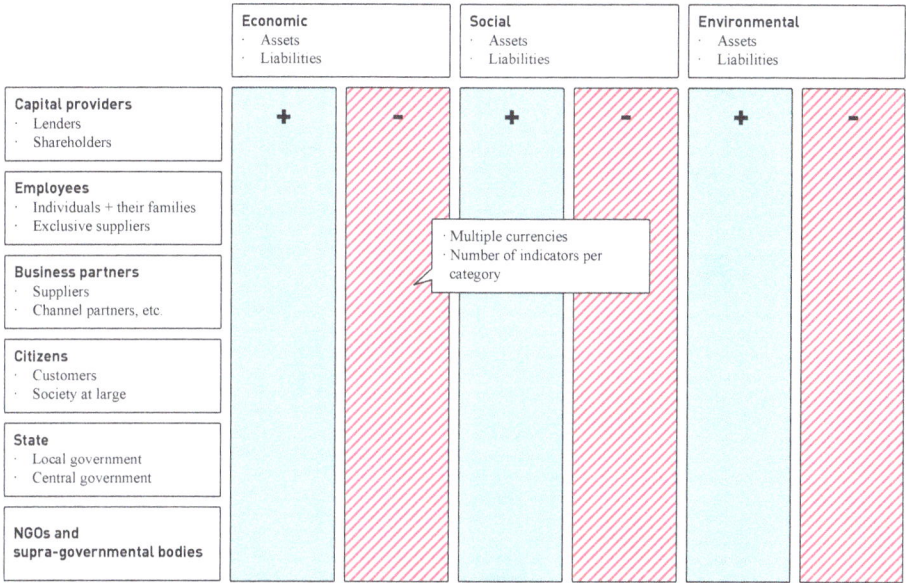

Figure 1.2: Schematic representation of the corporations' cost and contribution to society[20]

currencies, the measurement would be, in fact, less of a "balance sheet" and more of a "scorecard."

- *Approximately right rather than accurately wrong.* There is often a tendency to discard certain measures because there is no way to be accurate. For example, given that it is not possible to be accurate about the impact of *being* sustainable on sales, many companies do not measure it. We prefer to measure approximately what is relevant rather than giving those parameters an exact value of zero by discarding them.

- *Disaggregated metrics.* While aggregating results helps to make quick conclusions, we believe it is all too easy to make the wrong conclusions based on *aggregate* results. We also consider that the methodology should be able to provide insights into three types of dichotomies:

---

20. Source: VC2020 research.

Category	Economic		Social		Environmental	
	Assets	Liabilities	Assets	Liabilities	Assets	Liabilities
Capital providers	·EVA ·Interest	·Loss of share value ·Risk of default	·Education of shareholders about sustainable portfolios and long-term horizons			
Employee	·Salary ·Benefits	·Risk of lead firm not ensuring pension benefits ·Job losses during restructuring	·Career ·Self-esteem; personal advancement ·Social programs (schooling, healthcare, housing); sponsor art			
Suppliers and partners	·Revenues earned ·Knowledge/know-how transferred ·Pull due to lead firm products ·Supplier financing ·Assets provided by lead firm to partners	·Payment terms differential - lead firm working capital financing by suppliers ·Inability of channel partners to serve their customers due to lead firm supply chain problems	·Reputation earned from working with lead firm			
Customer	·Lead firm products making their lives easier ·Electricity costs savings	·Negative effects from low-quality products	·Health benefits from using lead firm products	·Negative effects from low-quality products (e.g. human suffering from low-quality healthcare products)	·Environmental benefits from using lead firm products	
Society at large	·Innovation which improves lives ·Progress - making more possible ·Number of jobs created ·Pull effect – investment		·Better quality of life (lighting making traffic safer or lower crime) ·For healthcare equipment: saving lives	·For example: for a lead firm in weapons business - loss of human life		·Cleaning up costs and environmental damages/waste ·However this is an economic benefit for suppliers who do this work
State	·Company and employee taxes ·Job creation in area	·Bribes? Lobbying? ·Subsidies paid to lead firm ·Tax evasion ·Divestments: unemployment benefits	·Pull effect – economic activity brought by lead firm leads to social development in the area => number of jobs for local people	·Bribes?	·Benefits from energy efficient products	·Overuse of limited resources, for example, water
NGOs and supra-governmental bodies	·License to operate for NGOs-in constructive collaboration scenario no need for NGOs		·Collaboration with business-shared value ·Improving labor conditions		·Value of information sharing-for example, company providing data to an environmental NGO on whale populations	

Table 1.1: High-level example[21]

Practice vs. performance. The methodology should look separately at practice (i.e. processes employed) and performance (i.e. actual results achieved by using certain practices)

- ***Leading vs. lagging indicators.*** Lagging indicators are metrics that measure end-state objectives or desired outcomes, while leading indicators are a set of metrics, which are predictive of the former.

- ***Supply chain vs. product/service specificity.*** We believe it is important to keep the *distinction* between cost and contribution to society, which is

---

21. Source: VC2020 research. Our classification of value (economic, social, environmental) has been inspired by John Elkington's *Triple Bottom Line: Profit, People and Planet.*

intrinsic to the corporation's product or service, and cost and contribution, which result from the company's supply chain.

Table 1.1 provides a high-level example of how the proposed framework for measuring the corporation's cost and contribution to society could be applied in practice.

Next steps

A key next phase for this project will include an iterative process of testing the proposed measurement tool and then fine-tuning it based on the findings from these tests. We anticipate that this work will be carried out in collaboration with several small businesses over the span of several months, and we are excited to report that we have already identified our first pilot partner.

Key takeaways

- Since the 2008 financial crisis, business leaders increasingly need to show how they create value for stakeholders along the entire value chain of their products or services, rather than just for shareholders. However, we still lack adequate measures of corporations' cost and contribution to society.

- Value measures are context dependent. We have therefore developed four future scenarios to help us understand how business leaders might need to measure their cost and contribution to society.

- Based on the insights from these scenarios, the VC2020 team proposes a new measurement framework structured as a balanced scorecard that can be adapted to any company in any given scenario.

- Two important principles for these measures are to consider the proportionality of the impact and cost in respect to the size of the company and to differentiate between leading and lagging indicators.

Chapter 2
Managing resource scarcities

Arjan van Weele
Luis Vivanco

Chapter 2
Managing resource scarcities

Arjan van Weele
Luis Vivanco

Executive summary

Managing resource scarcity is nothing new. Wars, natural disasters, the depletion of existing resources and geopolitics have all presented companies with scarcity issues for centuries. To survive, companies have historically used stockpiling and innovation to deal with these issues. It is only in the last few decades that resource scarcity management has become a strategic issue, driven mainly by concern over the enormous growth in demand for all types of products and services that has resulted from population and economic growth. Furthermore, some resources, such as water, land use, energy, raw materials and infrastructure, are correlated. Changes in the availability or demand of one can have ripple effects on the availability or price of another. This requires a comprehensive view of how to manage resources.

Research shows that, generally speaking, companies fall into two categories when it comes to the way they address long-term resource scarcity. There are those who believe that it is imminent and a matter of when rather than if. Then there are those with a radically different view who claim that resource scarcity is an overblown issue. They believe human ingenuity will either find new technologies that make a depleting resource obsolete and favor a more abundant one, or that new sources of any given resource will continue to surface. Both are at least partly right. Nevertheless, the short-term implications are the same for both, and only those companies with an effective resource scarcity strategy will thrive.

The supply and demand imbalance

In 2012, Dutch multinational Philips Electronics N.V. saw, in the span of a few months, a three-fold increase in the market prices of a category of raw materials of irreplaceable importance for the production of many of its products. Despite the price increase, continuous availability of the raw materials was far from certain. The culprits of the crisis were so-called rare earth elements (REEs), including indium, iridium and germanium, which are minerals used to manufacture many of the parts made by Philips, e.g. LEDs, solar cells, displays, LCDs, mobile phones, lasers, permanent magnets, fiberglass, solar cells and fuel cells. China was responsible for 97% of the world's REE production and, in previous years, it had put restrictions on the amounts it exported, prompting other countries to file a complaint with the WTO.[22] Independent studies[23] estimated that at the existing consumption rates, the world would run out of REEs in 100 years. While 100 years may seem like a long time, the struggle between increasing demand and available sources puts continuous pressure on sourcing specialists to find new sources of supply in order to prevent short-term material shortages and mitigate the ensuing price increases. According to a senior procurement executive, it was difficult to assess the gravity of the situation and what part of the shortage was due to an emotional component as companies afraid of stockouts rushed to purchase as much of those REEs as they could get their hands on pushing prices up anywhere from 10 to 100 fold. By the end of the year, availability improved and prices had gone back to or near their pre-crisis levels. To mitigate the heavy reliance on China, the US and other countries have stepped up their REE mining efforts.[24] This is expected to result in 20% of REEs production coming from outside of China by 2020.

But whether the crisis was real or manmade, it had a real impact on companies such as Philips, which saw not only its margins erode but also its operations in danger of coming to a halt.

22. Martyn, Paul. "Rare Earth Minerals: An End to China's Monopoly is in Sight." *Forbes*, June 8, 2012. <www.forbes.com/sites/ciocentral/2012/06/08/rare-earth-minerals-an-end-to-chinas-monopoly-is-in-sight/> (accessed August 6, 2013).

23. Cohen, D. 2007. "Earth's Natural Wealth: An Audit." *New Scientist*, May 23, 2007: 34–41.

24. Martyn, Paul. "Rare Earth Minerals: An End to China's Monopoly is in Sight." *Forbes*, June 8, 2012. <www.forbes.com/sites/ciocentral/2012/06/08/rare-earth-minerals-an-end-to-chinas-monopoly-is-in-sight/> (accessed August 6, 2013).

Raw material crises and their causes are hard to predict. Events such as the REE crisis help us understand the supply chain risks to which global companies are increasingly exposed.

Scarcity is, in essence, an imbalance in time and space between demand and supply of a given resource. It may be temporary in nature, structural in character or both. This chapter looks at the sources of scarcity and the challenges companies face when confronting them.

Global trends

The world's population is expected to increase 50% to 9 billion people by 2050. The growth will come mainly from developing countries, while developed nations will stabilize or, in some cases, show a decrease in population. Declining birth rates are the main factor contributing to the expected decline in developed countries, while access to fresh water, vaccines and food have reduced infant mortality rates and increased life expectancy, sometimes by as much as 25 to 30 years, in developing nations.

Demand for products and services

The impressive population and economic growth in developing countries will bring about a stronger middle class and result in an increase in demand for resources such as water, energy, food, raw materials and infrastructure.

The delivery of products and services in the volumes required to meet this increase in consumer demand will depend on the adequate provisioning of resources. We are already seeing a scarcity of many of these resources, and it is likely to increase in the future. The imperative for businesses and societies is clear; we have to learn to do more with less.

By itself, scarcity is going to call for new ways of operating businesses. First and foremost, strategies to secure resource availability to keep operations running must be developed and implemented. In doing so, companies will have to meet the written and unwritten rules demanded by governments and the communities they serve. The list of banned products in many countries (European countries being a prime example) is increasing and so are the legal requirements for full traceability of ingredients and components of consumer products. To meet the new requirements, companies are forced to look for alternative suppliers and production inputs in a narrowing worldwide resource base.

The changes in society are dictated by a more interconnected world. Social networks speed up the dissemination of information and influence society's values. In turn, societies are influencing legislation that addresses these values or creates de facto rules for the way they buy products and services. As they become wiser (and better informed), consumers in these societies demand better value and speedier product and service innovations. But consumers also require that companies be run in accordance with values that give priority to preserving the environment and improving the quality of life of not only the communities they serve but also the communities where they may source or produce.[25]

Scarcity may be caused by different factors, be they physical, as a result of a disaster or the exhaustion of natural resources, or geopolitical.[26] Whatever the causes, the consequences can be temporary in nature and their impact dependent on a company's ability to ensure the continuity of supply to its production lines, or they can be structural in nature, where the company must be prepared for alternative technologies or a shift in its business model. As we will argue, the availability of commodities such as water, energy, raw materials, food and land use and infrastructure are correlated, whereas dynamics in supply and demand precipitate price fluctuations of scarce materials.

Scarcity by type

Physical scarcity. At its most fundamental level, scarcity can relate to a lack of *availability*; a resource can simply exist in quantities too small to meet existing or future demand, or its reserves are dwindling while no new ones are discovered. While a material may be available, its extraction may be too

---

25. "Online Extra: Nike's New Game Plan for Sweatshops." *Bloomberg Businessweek*, September 19, 2004. <www.businessweek.com/stories/2004-09-19/online-extra-nikes-new-game-plan-for-sweatshops> (accessed August 6, 2013).

26. "Quick Scan: Natural Resources Risk." *CriticAnalytics*. <www.criticanalytics.nl/?page_id=1280#7> (accessed August 6, 2013).

costly or difficult to meet market demands. This is the case with many of the so-called rare earth elements, which exist throughout the world's regions but in concentrations too low to be economically feasible to extract. For this reason, the supply of REEs has been highly dependent at times on a few countries, notably China, where there is a high *concentration* of them. Other examples are certain food items such as vanilla and palm oil, and energy sources like gas and oil. Resource concentration can lead to a scenario where *distribution* in itself exacerbates the risks associated with supply continuity. Distribution of resources can rely on expensive infrastructure and logistics, be subject to restrictive environmental laws and natural disasters or be highly dependent on geopolitical issues.

Natural disasters. The tsunami that hit the northeastern coast of Japan in 2011 was an unforeseeable, once-in-a-lifetime event that had an immediate local effect on infrastructure, energy, food, water and raw materials, which directly disrupted the daily lives of millions of people over a vast region. But its ripples were also felt far beyond Japan's eastern shores as many nuclear power stations stopped operating as a preventative measure following the Fukushima station's meltdown. In a region that accounted for over a third of the world's production of highly specialized electronic components, industrial output was reduced, affecting customers around the globe.

The situation was similar to the Thailand floods the following year, where flooding and damaged port infrastructure disrupted the outward supply of food produce and electronic components such as hard disks. As these and other natural disasters like earthquakes or droughts show, *the reserves, production* and *distribution* of materials are all subject to their effects.

Geopolitics. A high geographical concentration of any commodity, particularly when it comes to food, energy (specifically oil and gas) and raw materials, will lead invariably to episodes where geopolitics become a factor. Geopolitics may take the shape of *export quotas, protection of resources for domestic demand* or, in an unintended way, lead to *political instability.* For example, under a long-standing treaty, Sudan uses 10% of the Nile's water while Egypt consumes about 80%. Less than 10% goes to seven upstream countries. A rise in demand will put pressure on how water resources are distributed,[27] which, in turn, will affect the political relationships among the nations involved.

Different resources are subject to different risks, as shown in *Table 2.1*. Some, like water, are less easily transportable over long distances and thus more prone to reserve concentration issues. Raw materials or energy availability, on the other hand, are much more prone to suffer from geopolitical crises.

	Physical			Disasters			Geopolitics		
	Reserves dsitribution	Production concentration	Abundancy	ND reserves	ND production	ND manufacturing	Stability of supplying countries	Export quota	Conflict minerals
Water	High	High		Medium		High			
Food / Land use	High	Medium	Low	High	High	Low		High	
Energy	High	High	High	High	High	Low	High	High	
Raw materials	High	Medium	High	High	Low	Low	High	High	High
Infrastructure		High						Low	

High risk   Medium risk   Low risk   Not Applicable

Table 2.1: Risk by type of commodity[28]

Implications for business: Why bother?

Be it due to physical depletion, natural disasters or geopolitical issues, and whether they are structural or temporary in nature, many companies are facing or will face resource scarcity in the future. PwC's research among 69 leading companies spanning seven industries and three regions shows that a majority of manufacturing firms consider resource scarcity to be a serious problem. The factors that the executives of these firms believe contribute to mineral and metal scarcity are shown in *Table 2.2*.

---

27. "East Africa Seeks More Nile Water from Egypt." *BBC News*, May 14, 2010. <http://news.bbc.co.uk/2/hi/africa/8682387.stm> (accessed August 6, 2013).

28. Source: VC2020 research.

Causes	High to very high impact	Medium impact	Total
Growing demand	65%	19%	84%
Geopolitics	54%	25%	78%
Extraction shortage	32%	41%	72%
Low substitution rate	38%	32%	70%
Re-use low	36%	29%	65%
Over demand (supercycle)	39%	23%	62%
Reserves run dry	30%	29%	59%
Insufficient R&D	25%	25%	49%

Table 2.2: Factors affecting resource scarcity[29]

The sources of scarcity present businesses with both an opportunity, in the shape of new products, substitutes and solutions and the chance to improve the way they operate, and a threat, as failure to address the issues derived from resource scarcity can lead to loss of competitiveness and high-cost disruptions of their operations. Companies that will thrive will be those that are able to adapt their business models, attain breakthrough innovations that circumvent resource limitations and develop supply chains that better respond to their needs. In the interim, business success will be determined by how much a company is able to control the supply of its scarce resources.

The recent popularity of biofuels will ease the dependence on fossil fuels in the short term for manufacturing, distribution and transport. However, as land use shifts from farming for food to crops destined for biofuels, the effects will be felt in terms of price increases for certain foods. Resource scarcity should not be seen as an isolated issue that affects only the resource in question be it water, a given mineral or natural gas, as resources are often interdependent. Hence, a change in one resource, be it price, availability or both, will manifest itself in others. *Table 2.3* depicts the interaction effects of some key resources.

In the intertwined world of resources, represented by *Table 2.3*, the most direct implications for businesses are the likely *disruption of the flow of critical production inputs* and *price fluctuations* that result from balance shifts

29. Source: Schoolderman, Hans and Rob Mathlener. "Minerals and Metals Scarcity in Manufacturing: The Ticking Time Bomb. Sustainable Materials Management." *PwC*, December 2011. <www.pwc.com/resourcescarcity> (accessed August 6, 2013). Figure 2.2 is reproduced with permission.

	Water	Land	Energy	Raw Materials	Infrastructure
Water		·Lower water availability has negative effect on crop yields, can make some crops unsuitable for areas. ·Changes in water management (dams, irrigation, etc.) can affect viability and productivity of land downstream. ·Dissapearance of water subsidies can have an effect on food prices.	·Water is a highly energy-intensive industry (energy = 40% of cost of water in developing countries). ·Groundwater depletion leads to higher energy use for extracting / desalinizing water.	·Water is used to extract minerals from rocks.	·Water is used as a raw material in construction.
Land	·Increased water use for irrigation can affect water resources (e.g., shrinking of Aral Sea). ·Land use change affects water management (e.g., wetland drainage reduces flood resilience).		·Agriculture is a major consumer of energy, both directly (cultivation, harvesting, processing, refrigeration, distribution) and indirectly (fertilizer, pesticides, other inputs).	·Use of land for agriculture reduces land for open-pit mining.	·Land use regulation will impact demand reducing infrastrucutre projects.
Energy	·Higher energy costs lead to higher water costs because of energy used in extracting / pumping / processing it. ·Water essential for hydroelectric power generation (c. 16% of global total power generation). ·Gas extraction through fracking and energy generation cooling contaminatets water sources.	·Higher energy prices lead to higher food prices as input and transport costs increase. ·Biofuels create an arbitrage relationship between food and fuel, pulling food costs upwards in line with energy. ·Biofuel cultivation leads to increase in demand for cultivable land. ·Deforestation for firewood.		·Mineral extraction is energy intensive - higher energy costs lead to higher costs.	·Increase energy demand will require power generation, transport and distribution infrastructure.
Raw Materials	·Extraction and refining of raw materials pollutes waterways.	·Open-pit mining takes away land used for agriculture.	·Raw materials extraction and processing are energy intensive.		·Increased demand in raw materials will require transport infrastructure (roads, bridges, ports, etc.).
Infrastructure	·Increase in water demand will require more infrastructural investment in dams, aquedcuts and distribution networks.	·Growth in infrastructure and urban sprawl reduces land used for agriculture. ·Alternative energy sources that rely on wind and solar power are land intensive.	·High growth rates in infrastructure projects and urban sprawl will increased energy demand.	·High growth rates in infrastructure projects and urban sprawl will increase energy demand.	

Table 2.3: Correlation between different commodity scarcities[30]

---

30. Source: VC2020 research.

between supply and demand. Many are already feeling the consequences of mineral and metal scarcity, as the study by PwC shows (see *Table 2.4*).

Industry	High to very high impact	Medium impact	Total
Renewable energy	33%	56%	89%
Infrastructure	45%	36%	82%
Energy & utilities	50%	29%	79%
Automotive	55%	18%	73%
Chemical	33%	33%	67%
High tech	44%	22%	67%
Aerospace	50%	0%	50%

Table 2.4: **Mineral and metal scarcity effect on different industries**[31]

Further analysis by McKinsey[32] shows how sharp price increases in commodities since 2000 have erased all the real price reductions of the 20th century.

Finally, based on the scenarios explored in the first chapter of this book (Theme 1: Measuring corporations' cost and contribution to society), it is very difficult to forecast the geopolitical conditions that will determine the market for resources, placing added importance on identifying critical resources that require action.

Identifying critical materials and resources

VC2020's research suggests three strategies to cope with materials and resource scarcities. These strategies are based upon the idea that resource scarcities represent significant risk, but also may provide significant opportunity for proactive companies. The suggested strategies are in line with the cradle-to-cradle concept, which is based on the idea of a circular economy.

When designing strategies for scarce and critical resources, a first step for companies is to identify their critical materials, i.e. those materials for

---

31. Source: Schoolderman, Hans and Rob Mathlener. "Minerals and Metals Scarcity in Manufacturing: The Ticking Time Bomb. Sustainable Materials Management." PwC, December 2011. <www.pwc.com/resourcescarcity> (accessed August 6, 2013). Figure 2.4 is reproduced with permission.

32. McKinsey Commodity Price Index.

which demand will outpace supply in the short and long term and for which no substitutes can be found. Next, these materials need to be analyzed for geopolitical resource effects based upon where the concentration of power (usually linked to resource concentration) is in a certain industry, which will determine long-term price increases and volatility (as shown in *Figure 2.1*).

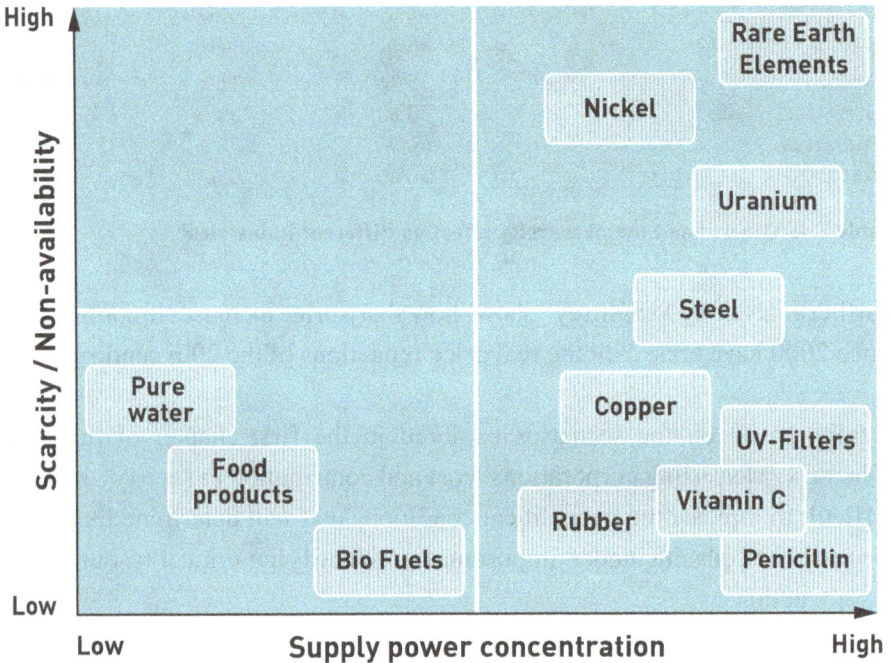

Figure 2.1: Strategic resource availability matrix[33]

Three resource strategies for the future

Three different sets of strategies can be developed to respond to resource scarcity:[34] 1) improving the availability of inputs, 2) enhancing the processes that reduce the dependency on such inputs or eliminating sources of risk and, finally, 3) minimizing the amounts of a resource needed employing the circular use of stocks.

_____

33. VC2020 research.

34. Quick Scan: Natural Resources Risk." *CriticAnalytics*. <www.criticanalytics.nl/?page_ id=1280#9> (accessed August 6, 2013).

1. ***Resource strategies*** *(stockpiling, multiple suppliers, vertical integration).* These include all strategies that aim to secure companies' future material needs through building buffer and security stocks, expanding the number of suppliers, building preferred relationships with critical materials' suppliers and backward integration, i.e. taking over suppliers of critical materials. The state-owned China Guangdong Nuclear Power Holding has followed this strategy by acquiring Australian based Extract Resources in 2012.[35] Swiss fragrance giant Givaudan has similarly invested in the farming of tropical plants that are critical to its business. In the aftermath of the Japan tsunami, Apple allocated a war chest of US$11 billion for safety stock of critical components and Philips started a program to reduce exposure to single suppliers. These companies not only secured critical materials and/or supplier resources, but they were also able to protect their supply position, improve their relative power in the supply chain and, hence, improve their business continuity and margins over their competitors.

2. ***Process strategies*** *(efficiency, substitution, relocation).* These include strategies aimed at reducing the need for critical materials through product and/or process redesign or reducing their criticality by *relocating* them. A Japanese manufacturer of beverage cans used aluminum more *efficiently*, thereby reducing its needs by 30% through an innovative stamp pattern without compromising strength. Through their global farmer development plans, both Nestlé and Unilever have been able to increase farmer productivity and obtain natural raw materials with more consistent quality at less volatile prices. In summary, using scarce resources more productively results in lower operational costs, slower depletion of natural resources and, when done right, more stable and secure future supplies. A global manufacturer of insulation fibers had production processes that were highly dependent on high-quality cokes that were in short supply and suffered high price volatility due to the existing supply being absorbed by the high growth of the Chinese economy. As its competitive position was endangered, its ingenuity pushed it to develop a new technology that *substituted* coal coke for other energy carriers (such as oil and gas) resulting in less dependency, lower cost and less price volatility.

---

35. "Chinese a Step Closer to Uranium Takeover in Namibia." *Mining Review.com*, January 16, 2012. <www.miningreview.com/node/20382> (accessed August 6, 2013).

3. ***Product strategies*** *(recycling, re-use, service)*. These strategies are aimed at coping with both short- and long-term scarcities. Companies need to think about their raw materials and components' cascade strategies. Recent research shows that less than 11.5% of the silver and 25% of the gold and palladium present in appliances are successfully recaptured.[36] Over 30% of copper disappears as waste and for antimony it is about 90%. For critical materials, such as bismuth, gallium, germanium, indium and scandium, the figure is over 99%. The "waste does not exist" approach used by Dutch-based Van Gansewinkel Group has allowed them to create a successful new business unit selling recycled glass and scarce metals through what they term "urban mining," which pertains to the harvesting of precious materials from waste collection. Similarly, pallet maker CHEP has made a business model out of refurbishing their widely recognized blue pallets so they can be used several times.

Conclusion

The outlook is heavily dependent on what your personal convictions may be, i.e. whether you believe that new discoveries and ingenuity will save the day or you are convinced scarcity is something that is only likely to worsen. Both arguments may be right, as empirical evidence has shown that scarcity skeptics are often right in minimizing impending doom scenarios. But history has also shown two more things. One, that short-term scarcities can have devastating effects on companies and their profitability and, two, that companies that fail to take into account and prepare for potential risk of resource scarcities will, unavoidably, suffer demise.

One way or the other, our message is clear; the world is only one or two steps away from the next resource crisis and global corporations that continue without a thorough revision of their global resource position do so at their own peril. It is imperative that they have a clear and comprehensive picture of their critical material needs and the suppliers that will provide for those needs. Once this is done, they need to develop specific resource strategies (based upon the Strategic Resource Availability Matrix). Failure to do this

---

36. Reijnders, L. 2012. "Raw materials Scarcity is Worse than Financial Crisis." *Financieele Dagblad*, July 18, 2012. (Dutch text.)

will put the fulfillment of their supply needs at risk and their ability to serve their global clients and markets in a continuous and efficient manner will be severely hindered. The future belongs to those companies that have the most effective resource strategy.

Key takeaways

- Demand for resources has increased at a fast rate in the last decades; a trend that will continue as populations grow and developing countries prosper.

- Resource scarcity may or may not be a paradigm-shifting event, as there is empirical evidence to support both premises.

- Short-term scarcities are unavoidable and their effects on prices and/or disruption to operations will affect more directly those companies that fail to implement adequate resource strategy measures.

- Resources are correlated and scarcity in one resource, be it structural or temporary, will produce changes in the price and availability of others.

Chapter 3
Scale and speed: Traditional multinationals versus emerging market firms

Howard Yu
Teresa Ferreiro

Chapter 3
Scale and speed: Traditional multinationals versus emerging market firms

Howard Yu
Teresa Ferreiro

Executive summary

For multinationals in the West, emerging markets represent both a growth story and, increasingly, the need for a pre-emptive strategy. Why? Because emerging-market firms have begun to display a clear pattern, they are focusing on customer market segments that are less attractive to – and therefore not satisfactorily served by – traditional multinationals. In addition, a poor country is usually surrounded by other poor countries. Once these firms secure a foothold in those markets, they begin to improve their product offerings at such a low cost that traditional multinationals find it difficult to replicate. The Japanese applied this strategy when the country began to take off almost 50 years ago. And there are a rising number of emerging-market firms in almost every industry imaginable that are keen to establish a foothold in the global marketplace.

The implications are clear. Emerging markets no longer represent additional market opportunities for traditional multinationals from the West. These markets are now home bases for a new breed of competitors. The "wait and see" approach often followed by many traditional multinationals is dangerously outdated. Some argue that Western multinationals need to master reverse innovation or emerging-market firms could destroy them. However, we believe that blindly following others is rarely effective. Instead, we argue that executives must first assess the fundamentals of their businesses before formulating a response and we offer a six-stage framework, which may be useful in doing this.

Emerging market firms go global

On April 17, 2012, China's SANY Heavy Industry made headlines when it completed its acquisition of German counterpart, Putzmeister, the world's leading manufacturer of concrete pumps. In the early 1990s, SANY focused on a homegrown concrete pump for transferring liquid concrete. The global market for this product was worth about US$5 billion a year and two German companies – Putzmeister and Schwing – dominated it, controlling over 90% of the market until around 2005. But in a dramatic industry shift, Putzmeister's sales fell from a record €1 billion in 2007 to a loss of €170 million in 2009. After buying Putzmeister for €0.5 billion, SANY became the sixth-largest heavy equipment manufacturer in the world, and the first in its industry in China to enter the FT Global 500 and the Forbes Global 2000 rankings.

Rather than buying Putzmeister just for access to its technology and manufacturing expertise, SANY aimed to make the company its overseas brand for concrete machines. The firm announced a €700 million sales target for Putzmeister for 2012 and a €2 billion target for 2016, essentially doubling Putzmeister's best sales figures.

This is one of the many examples of emerging market firms that are keen to establish a stronger global presence. So how can a once resource-poor, technologically backward company from a developing nation overtake one of the world's leading players? More importantly, what must traditional multinationals from the West do to avoid a fate similar to that of Putzmeister?

Key patterns of success among emerging market firms

Local businesses in emerging markets, usually by necessity, start out focusing on markets ignored by established multinationals. Rather than compete with cutting-edge technologies, they develop products and distribution systems for less affluent consumers. This strategy is not unique to the Chinese. Almost 50 years ago, the Japanese applied the same strategy when the country began to take off.

In the 1950s, Toyota set up its first overseas factory in Thailand and, by the time it entered the US, it had developed an extensive manufacturing and distribution network throughout Asia. But the firm designed vehicles for the muddy, slow, unpaved roads commonly found in many Asian countries including Japan. As a result, Toyota's first export to the US – the Toyota Crown, in 1957 – barely managed to crawl into Las Vegas after setting out from Los Angeles on what was planned to be a coast-to-coast endurance test across the country's vast highways. Toyota was thus forced to target secondary markets instead – housewives and teenagers who needed a second and/or affordable vehicle to run around town. Instead of hemorrhaging cash to develop the big cars typically sold in the US, Toyota spent the next couple of decades making subcompact cars that were popular in Asia and selected market segments of the developed world, allowing it to achieve greater economies of scale globally, while buying time to refine its skills in marketing and distribution.

By the late 1970s, Toyota's main foreign competitor, Volkswagen – best known for its Beetle – was mired in its own crisis. The strengthening of the deutschmark and higher production costs in Germany made Volkswagens prohibitively expensive in the US. As Volkswagen retreated, Toyota aggressively negotiated with US car dealers who were anxious to find alternatives. Leveraging its manufacturing scale advantages, Toyota was able to fill the gap in the product line with comparable models that cost almost 20% less.

Remarkably, Korean car manufacturers, including Hyundai and Kia have pursued the same strategy by initially producing subcompact cars, honing their skills in the low-end segment before moving upmarket.

Fast forward to China today. Haier, a homegrown electrical appliance company, began by making compact refrigerators for small homes in China, a market segment Western multinationals deemed unprofitable. Then, in the 1990s, Haier entered the US market, targeting a largely untapped group of consumers who would use its refrigerators in college dorms and hotel rooms. It has since captured almost half of that market segment. By 2009, Haier had surpassed Whirlpool as the world's top refrigerator producer by sales volume.

Let us step out of China and move west to India. Mahindra Tractors is the market leader for tractors in the country, serving local farmers. The company has developed a full line of small, reliable, rugged and fuel-efficient tractors that cost half the price of Deere's but are still enormously profitable. When Mahindra considered international expansion, it used its knowledge of small but rugged tractors to sell to the US and Australian hobby farming and golf course and lawn maintenance market segments. Hobby farmers typically own five acres or less, and landscaping firms offer landscaping and maintenance services to homeowners with large gardens. Customers in both these segments want tractors that are small, durable, easy to maintain and economical – just like the Indian farmers Mahindra Tractors serves at home.

The pattern is clear. Emerging-market firms that become successful tend to initially focus on a customer market segment that is less attractive to – and therefore not satisfactorily served by – traditional multinationals. In addition, a poor country is usually surrounded by other poor countries. A product that sells well domestically is likely to do well in neighboring countries. The resultant market size thus allows the local firms to achieve further economies of scale from its initially lower-cost structures. Having secured a foothold in those markets, these firms then begin to improve their product offerings at such a low cost that traditional multinationals find it difficult to replicate.

The implication? Emerging markets no longer represent additional market opportunities for traditional multinationals from the West. These markets are now home bases for a new breed of competitors. Latecomer companies that originate in emerging markets are increasingly competing head on with traditional multinationals in the global market, vying for the same customer segment. This shows that the "wait and see" approach among many traditional multinationals – i.e. wait for the rising incomes of the middle class in an emerging market to develop and then ship the firm's expensive, Western-looking products – is dangerously outdated. Companies must find ways to grow alongside with the hard-to-reach market segment in targeted emerging markets before it becomes too late.

Six stages of entering emerging markets

CEO Jeffrey Immelt at General Electric (GE) made a convincing case for Western multinationals to embark on what he termed "reverse innovation" – developing products in emerging markets and then distributing them globally. He argues that the conventional model that many Western multinationals have followed – developing high-end products at home in rich countries and adapting them for other markets around the world – is no longer sufficient because growth is slowing in many developed nations. If Western multinationals do not master reverse innovation, emerging-market firms could eventually destroy them.

The argument here is simple, compelling and elegant. Yet, executives must first assess the fundamentals of their businesses before formulating a response. Blindly following others rarely is effective. *Figure 3.1* presents a six-stage framework on how multinationals can enter emerging markets.

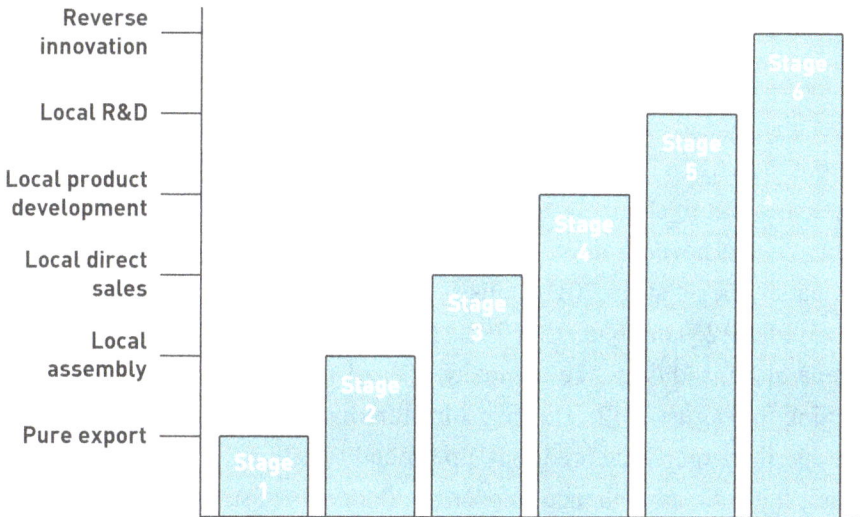

Figure 3.1: Six-stage framework on how multinationals enter emerging markets[37]

Stage 1: Pure export. When a domestic company exports its products outside the home country, it has taken the first step to becoming a global firm. A pure export model, however outdated it may seem, is still a common route for many

---

37. Source: VC2020 research.

global enterprises. It is particularly effective when the required sales volume for the company is small and the company can comfortably thrive with just a few niche markets around the world. Watchmakers such as Rolex and Patek Philippe largely rely on pure export. Occupying the ultra-top end of the luxury market, the two Swiss watchmakers compensate the small sales volume by putting an exorbitant price tag on their products.

Stage 2: Local direct sales. To retain the aurora of a premium image and expand the distribution network, companies may choose to build a direct presence in the local market. Prada, Gucci and many high-end fashion brands directly operate outlets around the world. This allows the company to control a consistent shopping experience, ranging from in-store ambience to merchandise display. When shopping inside a Giorgio Armani store, it can be hard to tell whether one is in Shanghai, Pudong or on Fifth Avenue in New York.

Lego, a Danish company famous for making colorful interlocking plastic bricks for children, has long exported its toys to China for the more affluent segment of the population. Historically, Lego mostly relied on third-party distributors to move products to independent retailers with little influence on product display and promotion. Separated by these middlemen, Lego could not reach out directly to its customers or gather market feedback. The complexity of these local retail channels also masked much market data (even as basic as merchandise turnover) and obscured business planning. Meanwhile, toy sales in China skyrocketed. In 2011 industry sales increased 45%, and, during the first half of 2012, sales had risen 75%. To ensure Lego was growing as fast as the general toy industry, the company opened its largest "experience store" in Beijing in August 2012. The flagship store had 300 square meters of floor space and the experience area took up around two-thirds of the store. Going forward, the company planned to open similar concept stores in other smaller Chinese cities to bring the Lego experience closer to home for the affluent population that was emerging in different parts of the country.

Stage 3: Local manufacturing. With the exception of the ultra-high-end fashion industry that is perpetually immune from low-cost competition, most companies – in the long run – need to take advantage of low-cost manufacturing outside their home country by leveraging the global supply chain. Flip over an iPhone and you will see "Designed by Apple in California, Assembled in China." (Tellingly, according to the *Wall Street Journal*, about 20% of Prada's collections – which range from bags and shoes to clothes for men and women – are now made in China.)

Offshoring is nothing new. But as these low-cost manufacturing hubs, such as China, India and Brazil, have ramped up their capabilities, more knowledge-intensive activities have also been offshored. In the PC sector, for example, contract manufacturers in Asia often take the leading role in product design and development, prototyping the latest laptops for clients such as HP and Dell. In the pharmaceutical industry, contract-manufacturing organizations such as China's WuXi AppTec provide a broad and integrated portfolio of laboratory and manufacturing services throughout the R&D process including support on clinical trials. WuXi's burgeoning client list includes some of the biggest industry giants such as Pfizer, Merck and AstraZeneca.

This is not a win-lose situation where research and development in the West is set for an inexorable decline. Rather, multinationals now have an unprecedented opportunity to rebalance their global R&D footprint, taking advantage of the differentiated capabilities across the world.

Stage 4: Local product development. To win in the emerging markets in a big way, some forward-looking multinationals have been pushing for localized product development. KFC, for example, is opening one restaurant daily on average (in addition to some 3,000 existing outlets), and expanding rapidly into small and mid-size Chinese cities. It has reinvented its menu and adjusted the flavor and spice in each region according to local tastes. It also owns a fleet of trucks and it has built its own warehouses to transport and store its products, a practice it shuns in other mature markets. A different kind of decentralization that allows local managers to experiment with new markets is required while remembering that the strategy deployed in the emerging market today is only ephemeral. The goal is to grow alongside the rising purchasing power of consumers, pushing standardization and realignment aside until later.

Similarly, Disney has discovered that Chinese parents who are unwilling to spend more than a few yuan for a movie will happily dip into their private savings to secure the best education for their children. So, in 2008 Disney China launched the first English learning center in a theme park environment in Shanghai. The curriculum, aimed at children between two and ten years old, was developed in the US and is taught by native English-speaking trainers. It proved so popular that within three years it had expanded to more than 30 centers around the country. Disney did not simply adapt its existing products from the US for a Chinese audience. To win big in China, Disney had to move into a completely new product category for the local population.

Stage 5: Local research. Increasingly, traditional multinationals are setting up advanced research laboratories in emerging markets. Novartis, GlaxoSmithKline and Johnson & Johnson have all pronounced an "in China for China strategy." To be sure, the conventional logic for such a move may still be true. In China and India, biology and chemistry PhDs are usually abundant, patient enrollment rates for clinical trials are high, labor costs are low and tax concessions are generous.

However, these newly set up research centers are also expected to focus on discovering and commercializing large-scale prevention and treatment regimens for diseases commonly found in the emerging economies. Because of the different climatic conditions, dietary habits, living standards and lifestyle, disease classes vary greatly across geographic regions. In China, infectious diseases such as hepatitis, tuberculosis, syphilis, dysentery, gonorrhea and foot-and-mouth still wreak havoc. Effective treatments targeting unique molecular pathways for gastric and liver cancer that are commonly observed in the region are also waiting to be identified.

The impetus for multinationals to build a deep bench for their research arms in emerging markets extends also into other knowledge-intensive industries. The IBM China Research Laboratory (CRL) in Shanghai, set up in 1995, has long supported product development efforts around the world, leveraging its low-cost structure and focusing on the more labor-intensive, routine assignments. But over time, CRL has acquired higher-level capabilities, helping IBM win major contracts in the country, and in the process, shedding its former role and image. When China rolled out the 3G platform nationally, CRL partnered with China Telecom to develop infrastructure that utilized a different radio interface mandated by the central government, putting IBM ahead of other European and American telecom providers when competing in the Chinese market.

Stage 6: Reverse innovation. Multinationals operating in stages 4 and 5 explicitly recognize that if a firm is to succeed in emerging markets it must innovate for them. But excitingly, innovations developed for emerging economies can be extended back to rich countries, thereby opening new business possibilities not previously available.

Jeffrey Immelt recalled that GE's ultrasound business had established a solid market position in rich countries around the world as early as 2000.[38] Its wheelbase systems, targeting well-funded hospitals in the West, emphasized performance, speed and image quality through cutting-edge technologies. Businesses in developing countries, where price matters most, followed by portability and ease of use, had been disappointing to GE. Led by the then head of the global ultrasound business, Omar Ishrak, a special team in China was given complete autonomy to build a compact ultrasound machine from scratch to fulfill local requirements. Meanwhile, important R&D resources at the corporate level were made available to the local team including seconding three of the company's best and most respected engineers from Japan, Israel and South Korea full time for months.

The model was sold for just US$15,000, less than 15% of GE's high-end ultrasound machines. It was an instant hit in rural clinics, where doctors used it for simple applications, such as spotting enlarged livers and gallbladders and stomach irregularities. While the portable machine became the growth engine of GE's ultrasound business in China, the product went on to generate new growth in rich countries. Billed as a handheld, pocket-sized device that visualizes the inside of a patient's body before going into a hospital, physicians at doctors' clinics or paramedics at accident sites found the compact machine enabled them to deliver better services, such as diagnosing pericardial effusions (fluid around the heart) and other pre-screening. By targeting new applications

---

38. For an excellent account of GE Healthcare Business in China, please consult: Immelt, Jeffrey R., Vijay Govindarajan and Chris Trimble. "How GE Is Disrupting Itself." *Harvard Business Review*, October 2009. Govindarajan, Vijay and Chris Trimble. *Reverse Innovation: Create Far from Home, Win Everywhere*. Boston: Harvard Business Press, 2012.

where portability is critical, this ultrasound device engenders little risk of cannibalization for GE's high-end machines. In the words of Immelt, "reverse innovation isn't optional; it's oxygen" for future growth.

The impetus for growth, the importance of emerging markets

Emerging markets represent both a growth story and, increasingly, the need for a pre-emptive strategy for multinationals. Multinationals must not only successfully leverage their existing product offerings for the matching market segments found in emerging markets for incremental growth, but also turn their emerging market operation into a growth platform to capitalize on business opportunities around the world.

Of course, a strategy shift does not happen overnight. The evolution of CEVA logistics – a leading logistic provider headquartered in the Netherlands – shows us how a firm shifts its emphasis by making small bets on where the growth is along the way.

CEVA entered China in 1988 and along with a local company, Anji, formed the first automotive partnership in the country. As a first mover, CEVA was ahead of the competition in building a reliable network of local partners to deliver products on time to cities in every tier (i.e. cities of all sizes) throughout China. Years later, as many Western companies were clamoring for business opportunities in China, they found themselves needing logistic partners that could not only "move boxes around" but also that could help restructure their distribution channel for greater efficiency. In 2010, Sony worked with CEVA to create its first e-commerce platform in China, with a built-in track-and-trace function that could locate shipments from its central warehouse to final customers. Bypassing the highly fragmented third-party distributors, Sony was able to achieve a level of transparency of its logistic information that it otherwise could not obtain.

But CEVA did not limit itself to serving international clients. It also aggressively marketed itself to local giants that were expanding abroad. Huawei, a leading communication technology provider, had been growing steadily since its founding in 1997. By 2005, Huawei was so successful that, in order to meet its market demand, the firm had to outsource many of its non-core functions. Showing a great deal of flexibility, CEVA expanded into a new range of services targeting local companies for services, such as assembling and packaging, on top of leveraging its existing global network to help clients expand abroad. Going forward, CEVA aimed to develop localized products that targeted small- to medium-size enterprises in China as many of these aspiring companies were vying to expand on a regional basis. In the words of a veteran of CEVA's China operation:

We must grow alongside the emerging national champions. If we don't, some local logistics suppliers will become our formidable competitors tomorrow.

Key takeaways

- Successful emerging-market firms tend to initially focus on a customer market segment that is normally not served by traditional multinationals because it is less attractive to them.

- A product that sells well domestically in an emerging country is likely to do well in its neighboring countries where social and environmental factors are usually similar. The resultant market size thus allows local firms to achieve economies of scale. Having secured a foothold in those markets, these firms then begin to improve their product offerings from a cost structure that is so low that traditional multinationals find it difficult to replicate.

- Emerging markets no longer represent additional market opportunities for traditional multinationals from the West. These markets are now home bases for a new breed of competitors. The "wait and see" approach adopted by some Western firms can be very dangerous.

- Entering emerging markets is no longer an option for most traditional multinationals from the West – it is now a must.

Chapter 4
Optimizing IT-enabled processes and systems in the value chain: The role of governance

Michael Wade
Bettina Büchel
Arjan van Weele
Christopher Zintel

Chapter 4
Optimizing IT-enabled processes and systems in the value chain: The role of governance

Michael Wade
Bettina Büchel
Arjan van Weele
Christopher Zintel

Executive summary

IT-enabled processes and systems are widely acknowledged as key drivers of global value chain management. When investing in these processes and systems, corporations want to benefit from standardizing their worldwide networks, but they are faced with the challenge of how to adapt to and support differentiated markets and business models with standardized solutions. The goal of this chapter is to understand the implementation journey to IT-enabled processes and systems in global corporations and to provide insights into the governance challenge of balancing centralization versus localization.

The four lessons presented in this chapter: top management support is critical: push and pull; on-going governance has to be responsive; standardization must be executed in the right sequence; and getting local support requires skillful interface managers, represent a set of best practices that increases the odds of successfully moving from a siloed organization to one that can effectively balance local and global needs. Achieving efficiency gains while still being responsive to local needs requires careful management of process and system standardization. Although it is a long and difficult journey, our research shows that through careful consideration of governance practices, companies can realize the optimal point of standardization and implement IT-enabled processes and systems that lead to higher performance levels.

Standardization vs. adaptation: Balancing local flexibility and global efficiency[39]

We state that we are a global company with operations in multiple countries. So, from the outside, it looks like a true multinational; but the view from the inside is less clear: we have four e-mail systems, 13 billing systems, each of our plants works in a different way, and we are miles away from having a single view of the customer.

Over the years, we have been told countless versions of the above story. But recently, we have started to hear a new story, which goes something like this:

We have just gone through seven years of process standardization and we've implemented an ERP system to gain global efficiencies, but now it feels as if we have gone too far. Sure, we have a better view of the business and we have gained benefits through common processes, but we seem to have lost some of our competitive edge. We're just not as agile or customer-oriented as we used to be.

These stories illustrate a central dilemma faced by many large organizations: how to balance local flexibility and global efficiency. Yet, our research has shown that some firms have managed to implement strategies that are both locally agile and globally efficient. The optimal balance, however, between local flexibility and global efficiency seems highly dependent on the context in which a firm operates as well as a firm's particular strategic direction.

For most companies, the IT standardization journey begins in the "silo" quadrant (see *Figure 4.1*). Strong business silos – represented by business units, geographical markets, functions or lines of business – emerge when there is a high degree of local autonomy and a low degree of global control. This governance structure allows firms to gain an in-depth understanding of local market needs and the ability to meet those needs through customized, locally developed or adapted solutions. As firms grow, however, this approach

39. This chapter is based on our research and analysis of 20 interviews with senior IT and operational managers at 12 global companies as well as secondary data collected from public sources. We thank the 20 senior IT and operational managers who provided the insights, which greatly assisted our research. We also thank Irene Kamp for her research work as part of the VC2020 project.

becomes increasingly inefficient. The low standardization level across the silos, leads to costly duplication of IT-investments and maintenance or process inefficiencies. More seriously, the structure of each silo inhibits the exchange of information and best practices, so that the global "sum" of the organizational expertise is little more than the sum of the individual parts.

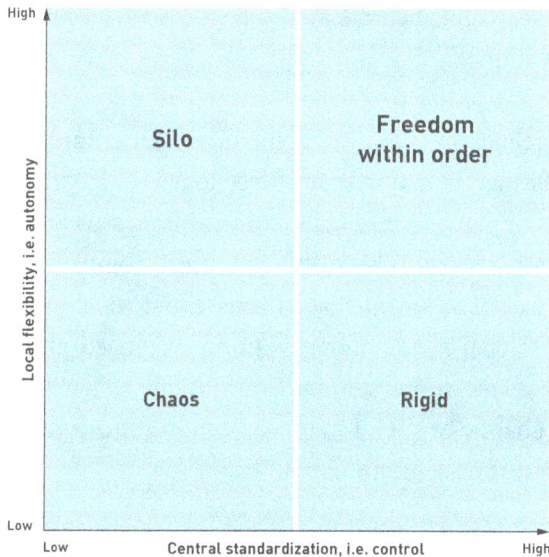

Figure 4.1: The challenge of IT standardization[40]

To overcome the limitations and dilemmas of this structure, organizations turn to company-wide standardization programs to increase the level of global efficiency. Since these tend to disrupt and threaten local processes, systems and autonomy, organizations often end up in the "chaos" quadrant, where individual business units need to give up many of their legacy systems and processes, often at a stage where sound alternatives have not yet been fully adopted. The length of time that business units stay in this quadrant depends on a number of factors, such as the extent of the transformation, the amount of local resistance to change and the quality of the change management process.

After this period of disruption and uncertainty, sometimes referred to as the "shakeout period," firms enter the "rigid" quadrant. We have observed

---

40. Source: VC2020 research.

an increasing number of organizations that have entered this stage and gone through enterprise system implementations and process improvement programs such as Six Sigma and Lean Manufacturing. They have managed to cut down on process and system duplication, improve economies of scale and scope and become more effective at sharing information, knowledge and best practices across the organization. However, there is an increasing tendency among these firms to fall behind in key areas, such as local responsiveness, agility and innovation.

To avoid the bureaucracy liability, companies can complete the journey by evolving towards the final quadrant, "freedom within order," characterized by corporations that have hybrid standardized processes and IT solutions that allow more customization. Within this quadrant, companies maintain global efficiency and control where it makes sense, and re-acquire a high level of responsiveness to local needs, along with an enhanced ability to change. In other words, they lose some standardization and efficiency gains, but they don't return to a chaotic or siloed state. As seen in *Figure 4.2*, companies often fail to follow a direct path to "freedom."

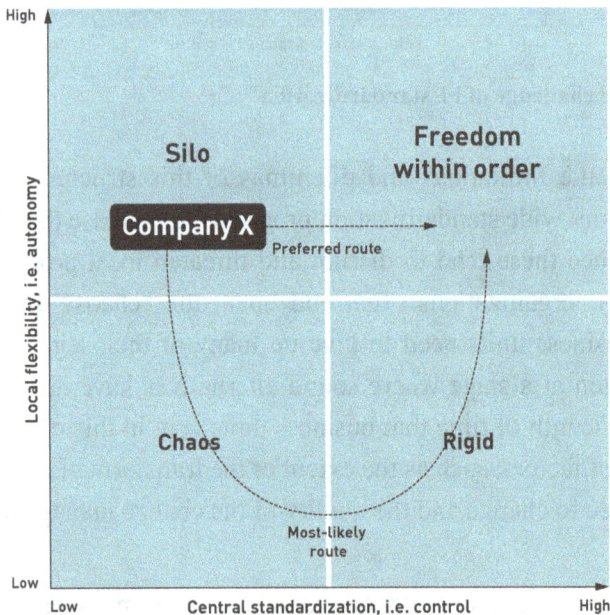

Figure 4.2: Common routes to "freedom"[41]

---

41. Source: VC2020 research.

Achieving global efficiency does not come without costs. Many firms become bureaucratic and inflexible and they are slow to innovate. Every case we encountered, even those that were ultimately successful, passed through the "chaos" quadrant. All global efficiency programs will encounter two challenges. First, they require a change to many organizational processes and systems, which leads to significant disruption. Second, they have to overcome substantial resistance from local markets and units that are affected by the change. Either of these challenges can derail the efficiency journey.

Corporate governance is a key contributing factor for a successful journey from a siloed structure to one that is more globally efficient. The purpose of strong governance is threefold. First, it ensures that there is a mechanism to decide which processes and systems should become the global standard. Second, it provides a mechanism for exceptions to the standard to be identified and authorized. Strong and clear governance is critical to ensure that the right balance of these elements is established and maintained over time. The third purpose of governance is to identify processes or systems that should be discontinued because they do not fit the global template.

Poor governance can lead to a set of processes and systems that are either too large or too small. The standard set can become too large if it is full of redundant systems and rarely used or duplicate processes. In such cases, an organization might appear to be globally rationalized, but upon closer inspection, its bloated core makes it bureaucratic, inefficient and slow. Perhaps the firm has standardized on SAP enterprise software, but because of infighting, standard software applications are customized. Hence, many of the benefits of scale are lost. If the standard set is too small, the organization may never completely leave the silo quadrant. Too many local exceptions can easily downgrade the benefits of a global standard. In most cases, the local versus global dilemma essentially comes down to a question of when to do the same things the same way and when to allow things to vary.

The journey towards balancing global efficiency and local responsiveness

Based on our research and analysis, we offer four lessons for organizations wishing to find an effective balance between global efficiency and local responsiveness.

Lesson 1: Top management support is critical: Push and pull

Any large-scale standardization or IT system implementation initiative will inevitably encounter resistance at the local unit level. Be cautioned! We have observed that it can take substantial time to find the right local and global balance – a timeline for which the financial markets will likely have little patience. In the case of one of our subject companies, the still-incomplete efficiency journey started more than 10 years ago. Overcoming resistance requires time and patience, particularly from influential markets or business units. We have observed that strong top management commitment is critical for implementation success and, conversely, the lack of this visible support leads to sub-optimal results or failure. One interviewee echoed this view:

My predecessor in the chief information officer (CIO) role didn't want to battle regions on many of the standardization initiatives. This was fine and perhaps the right move for the time. Then, we got a new CEO, who had a vision to build a truly global company. He believed that this was only possible with a high degree of standardization. Since then, we have been moving ahead quickly. Support from the CEO is critical.

Before an initiative was introduced to improve an oil and gas company's global operations and connectivity through a common platform, there had been no mandate from the top for change from an IT implementation perspective; the process was voluntary. The implementation of this initiative, however, was supported by a clear mandate from top management. As the deploy and continuous improvement manager of contracting and procurement (CP) systems and processes recalled:

In earlier years, during the process of regional harmonization, there was no mandate for change ... This was different at the outset of this initiative, as everyone had to agree on one design, which we planned for and which we rolled out everywhere.

The initiative succeeded because it achieved buy-in and support from business unit leaders and local managers. CP had clearly communicated the message that this standardization was going to happen, and most country managers understood the potential benefits. The implementation team, even with the CP leadership backing it, talked to and invested in people throughout the organization, engaging stakeholders and actively driving adoption of the initiative's platform.

Top management sponsorship of an initiative by a large consumer goods company to adopt common business processes and IT systems around the world that allowed each market to make specific analyses and local decisions, required a critical "push" to get the project off the ground. "[The former CEO's] sponsorship was a key success factor for the initiative," explained the head of the company's digital strategy. Top managers communicated that the initiative was not "just another" system or process exercise but was critical to the global organization's continued success. Additionally, there were supportive market heads that served as champions. These champions quickly understood that the initiative would provide the richness of data that was needed to compete in a globalized world. Market heads also realized that the initiative meant that their supply chains could be fully traced and tracked. This proved to be of great value when a food safety issue was uncovered. The company was able to react because it knew where its raw materials were sourced from and how these were consumed in all stages of the company's supply chain. Overall, successful pilots and support from top management as well as top regional managers were critical to creating momentum and shifting mindsets throughout the organization that led to the initiative's success.

It should be noted that after a period of time, we noticed that strong top management commitment became less important. Companies moved from a "push" scenario, where changes were mandated, to more of a "pull" scenario, where units requested the changes. At this point, the benefits of the standardization journey became more apparent and units began accepting the solution.

Lesson 2: On-going governance has to be responsive

Strong and clear governance is critical to ensure that the right balance of core processes (standardized across the company), edge processes (some customization is allowed) and non-authorized processes are established and maintained over time. Not only should governance help determine whether a process or system is core, edge or not authorized, but it should also provide a mechanism for moving from one process category to another. These movements are critical for responding to changes in the business environment. Indeed, the external environment may require changes to the proportion of core and edge elements. For example, some core elements might no longer be considered strategically important, and thus may be jettisoned from the core. As seen in *Figure 4.3*, an edge element that becomes more strategically important over time, like the management of risk associated with exposure to social media, might move into the core element set.

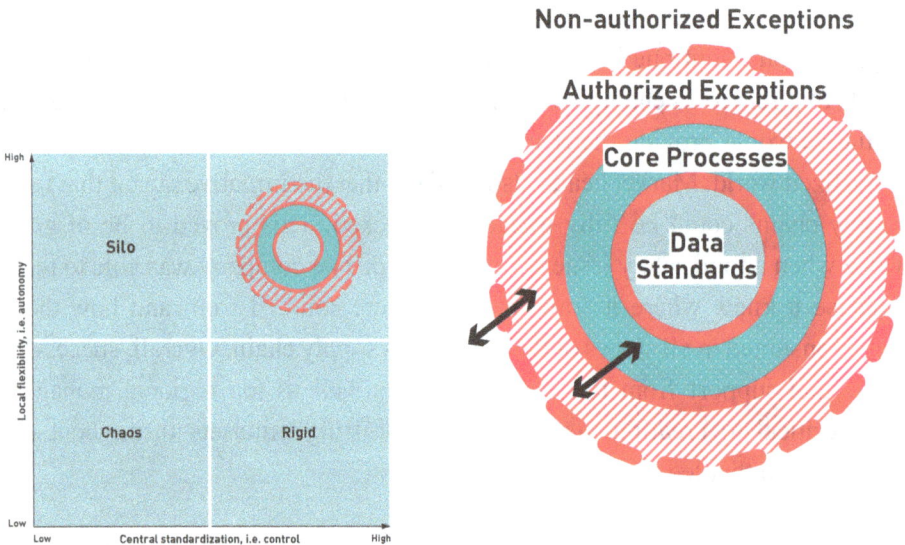

Figure 4.3: **Governance and maintaining balance between fixed and floating elements**[42]

A CIO suggests that these initiatives can be conceptualized as an onion (see *Figure 4.4*). Every time you remove a layer, you get closer to the core. Inside the core you will find all the process tools for finance, manufacturing, part of HR and supply chain management. On the outer layers you will find variances as the system becomes more flexible for customer and commercial objectives as a result of customizable plug-ins.

---

42. Source: VC2020 research.

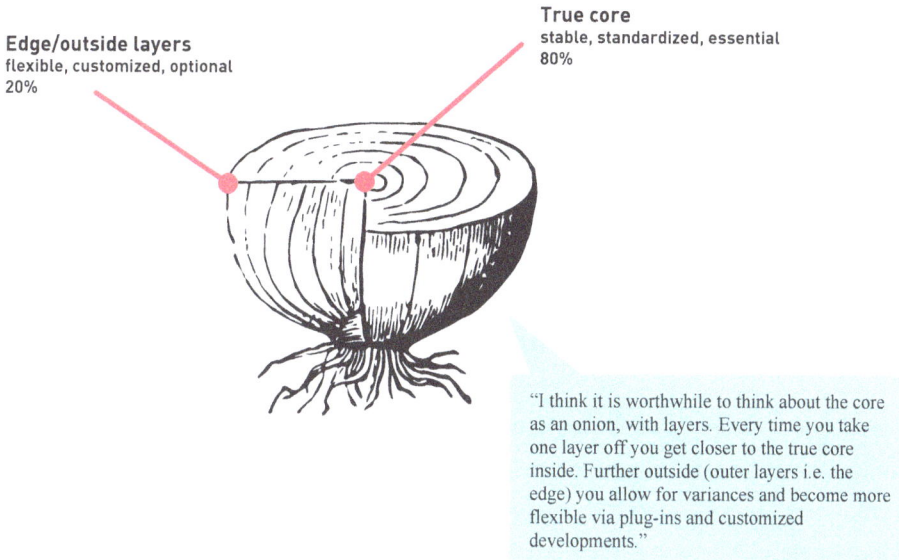

Edge/outside layers
flexible, customized, optional
20%

True core
stable, standardized, essential
80%

"I think it is worthwhile to think about the core as an onion, with layers. Every time you take one layer off you get closer to the true core inside. Further outside (outer layers i.e. the edge) you allow for variances and become more flexible via plug-ins and customized developments."

Figure 4.4: The "onion" diagram

The CIO explained that an exception or edge solution would be considered in three different situations: when the process or system is not contrary to the company's best practice; when there is a clearly demonstrated need; and when there is a possibility to use the process or system in another market. If all these conditions are in place, then an exception may be approved, and it could eventually become part of the standard core. Additionally, there was a set of "authorized edge solutions," which was not part of the centralized core but was vetted and used by multiple markets. Careful management of these authorized edge solutions allowed markets to learn from each other. An example of such a solution is the distributor management system in Malaysia and Singapore. The initiative team found that this system was too complicated and expensive for the Indian market. In response, a basic solution was put in place in India, which had proved its value in Indonesia and Ghana.

According to the process owner and general manager of CP systems and processes at a large oil and gas company, it is important to allow for some flexibility in the edge processes, even within a fairly standardized environment like CP. When there was a specific business reason to integrate a specific local tool within SAP, e.g. an IT solution that would allow the individual business unit to comply with local laws and regulations, the company did so. Consequently, managing the interfaces becomes a challenge.

In the multinational companies that we observed, governance was usually provided through a combination of head office staff, functional leaders and individuals at the interface between the business and IT. In order to make this triangle work, effective governance is a key requirement.

Lesson 3: Standardization must be executed in the right sequence

The first phase of the implementation journey should revolve around understanding in detail how processes are managed across the organization. The evaluation and rationalization of organizational processes should precede any large-scale IT system implementation project. In the case of a consumer goods company, SAP was implemented only after the process landscape was clearly mapped and understood. According to a key member of the implementation team:

We started looking at the end-to-end processes, 37 major process groups in all (e.g. HR hire to retire, order to cash). All processes were then deconstructed to five levels. On the fifth level, you are one-on-one with system transactions. On levels three to four you could already tell how the market operates. Then we analyzed the alignment between the markets' processes and the global best practice processes. When we identified a mismatch, we had to decide which one to take and which one to change.

A common temptation is to move too quickly into system implementation mode without first having a full understanding of the process landscape. One of our sample organizations that lost patience with the SAP implementation, decided to fast track the process-mapping stage and simply overlay the software on top of existing processes. After seven years, the project showed few gains and the company is currently considering scrapping it altogether and re-starting the initiative.

A large oil and gas company that maintained a process-led approach underwent extensive integration projects that strengthened the structure and methodology of the global approach. According to one executive:

We spent the first few years documenting the functional processes, discussing the procurement channels, lean workshops, etc. in order to make the design. That is, however, only the starting point. The implementation then takes time and requires phasing the system rollout. We couldn't have succeeded without having standardized processes and data in place.

Once processes are well understood and appropriately standardized and once data formats are streamlined across the organization, then large-scale IT system implementation can begin (see *Figure 4.5*). We found that following this progression was strongly linked to a successful transition from quadrant 1 (silo) to quadrant 3 (rigid). Cases in which this sequence was not followed tended to languish for longer in quadrant 2 (chaos).

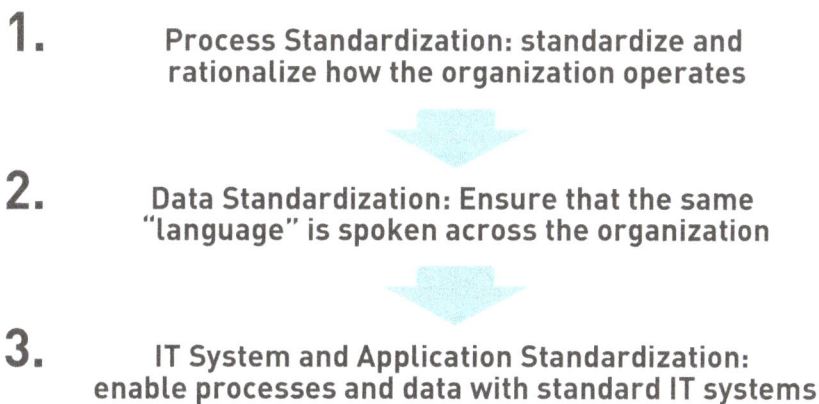

1.   **Process Standardization: standardize and rationalize how the organization operates**

2.   **Data Standardization: Ensure that the same "language" is spoken across the organization**

3.   **IT System and Application Standardization: enable processes and data with standard IT systems**

Figure 4.5: Process standardization sequence[43]

An additional factor that is an important component of a successful efficiency journey is the correct sequencing of organizational functions. After completing the process standardization sequence outlined in *Figure 4.5*, companies should begin to implement the new standardized processes and systems in a defined order. See *Figure 4.6* for a comparison of three functional clusters and the order in which the process and system implementation has occurred in the successful cases.

---

43. Source: VC2020 research.

1.   **Back office functions**
- Procurement
- Finance
- Accounting

2.   **Ensuring Supply functions**
- Operations
- Logistics
- Inventory

3.   **Generating demand functions**
- Sales
- Marketing

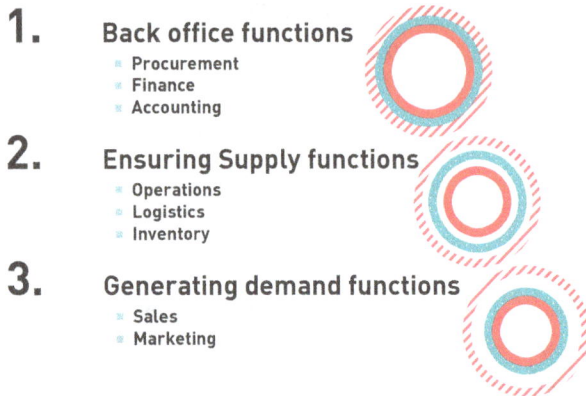

Figure 4.6: Functional sequencing[44]

Firms that tend to have successful outcomes begin with back office functions, like accounting, finance and procurement. These functions are typically process driven and have the most to gain from standardization and efficiency programs. Moreover, the proportion of fixed processes is likely to be high and floating exceptions correspondingly low. By comparison, market facing functions, including business development, marketing and sales, tend to require more floating processes and are likely to be the most resistant to change. Starting with these functions can be a recipe for disaster. In the example of a coffee company, all processes up to and including warehousing (procurement, manufacturing, etc.) were highly standardized, while those that were downstream of the warehouse were highly variable, as the "digital age" required a higher level of interaction with consumers. According to one of our partner CIOs:

We started with finance, HR, IT and purchasing. These were standardized and centralized. They were part of a program to reduce costs and increase efficiencies. We did not tackle the differentiating processes right away, such as shop-floor automation, order management, pricing and sales. These areas required flexibility and different degrees of standardization.

Lesson 4: Getting local support requires skillful interface managers

Given that the success of an individual business unit often rests on its ability to adapt and respond to local demands, the desire by headquarters to push

---

44. Source: VC2020 research.

through efficiency and standardization programs may not always be welcomed: it can easily lead to passive or active resistance. For instance, a business unit may only ceremonially adopt a new practice, since it does not believe in the economic benefit of the practice within its local context. Alternatively, the unit may intentionally decide not to implement the practice while reporting otherwise to headquarters. In the extreme, a subsidiary with a strong power base could actively defy or obstruct corporate headquarters and take independent action, resulting in non-adoption of the new system or practice. Defiance is likely to occur when the norms and interests of the local organization diverge substantially from the center. Faced with contradictions and misalignment between local and global interests, organizations must determine how to get the commitment of local units to fully implement a new global practice or IT solution without compromising adoption.

It is important for managers to realize that the journey toward standardization is an iterative process that happens over a long period of time. The journey will include sometimes making difficult decisions on what is an essential core process and what is an adaptable authorized edge process. These decisions could lead to a leap backward and lower standardization in the short term in favor of realizing higher standardization and greater values in a long-term leap forward (see *Figure 4.7*).

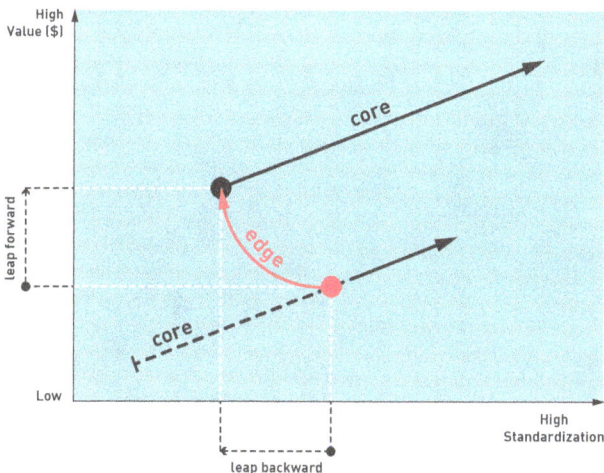

Figure 4.7: Long-term leap forward[45]

---

45. Source: VC2020 research.

Key takeaways

- Leaders must balance efficiency and flexibility to achieve high performance in dynamic environments. Achieving efficiency gains while still being responsive to local needs requires careful management of process and system standardization. The governance process is a key determinant of implementation success.

- The four lessons presented in this chapter represent a set of best practices that increases the odds of successfully moving from a siloed organization to one that can effectively balance local and global needs.

- It is a long and difficult journey. Through careful consideration of governance practices, our research shows that companies can realize the optimal point of standardization and implement IT-enabled processes and systems that lead to higher performance levels.

Chapter 5
The organizational design shift

Teresa Ferreiro
Emanuela Zappone-Fabre
Carlos Cordón

Chapter 5
The organizational design shift[46]

Teresa Ferreiro
Emanuela Zappone
Carlos Cordón

Executive summary

Over the past years, organizations have evolved from being very independent and internally focused to becoming part of an ecosystem that includes the entire value chain. The high level of outsourcing and specialization has resulted in companies having interdependent relationships with the other companies in the value chain. While the focus continues to be mainly internal and on the customer, it is starting to move towards the ecosystem that serves and manages the whole value chain (with the client serving as a prime driver).

This change implies that traditional organizational structures with their business units, geographic structures or other models, need to be adapted to consider the whole ecosystem. The challenge is how to organize and structure the management of the value chain, from supplier to customer.

This change will not only affect the structure but also the leadership competencies required by the executives who manage those value chains. In fact, many top executives express concern about finding leaders with the right competencies in their organizations. Hence, this topic became a VC2020 research stream.

Our research has explored the future concerns and organizational design and leadership trends of a number of companies in the VC2020 Center. This chapter

46. Part of the content in this chapter is based on an unpublished dissertation by Emanuela Zappone.

presents a business and organizational design model and a five-step process to implement that design shift.

The organizational design shift

Introduction

Chapter 2 of this book helped us understand how critical the value chain is for companies, particularly big multinationals. When unexpected events affect the value chain, their impact is not always obvious, so companies often do not consider if and how they will affect them and their suppliers.

When the tsunami hit the coast of Japan, many companies reviewed their value chains and were relieved because they thought that none of their factories or their suppliers' factories was in the affected area. Time blew away this confidence. It only took a couple of days for these organizations to realize the direct impact of the tsunami across their production lines. All of Japan suffered power shortages. Factories located miles away from the hot spot were unable to produce and deliver at their normal speed. Who could have foreseen this situation? In some cases, the companies' direct suppliers were not located in Japan, so they thought they were safe. Unfortunately, for many companies, the supply chains of their suppliers had operations in Japan, which affected the delivery of their final product. What initially seemed to be happening miles away from the reality of many organizations, ended up causing major disturbances around the globe.

Corporations handled the crisis in a variety of ways. One option was to accept the losses caused by production shortages, try to adapt to the situation and survive until things got back to normal. Another option that Philips chose[47] was to create a team specifically responsible for managing the crisis and tracking the situation by the minute. Apple opted for a more extreme resolution. Before collecting the information to understand the impact of the event and state of their value chain, they decided to immediately spend US$11 billion buying

---

47. For more information, refer to Cordón, C. and Vivanco, L. *Philips Japan (A)*. IMD case no. IMD-6-0333, 2013.

all the available stock they might need, "just in case" their ecosystem was somehow affected.

The tsunami brought with it the realization that companies are more deeply linked to their suppliers than they thought. Keeping control over relationships with their direct suppliers did not ensure success. In fact, what it really showed was that companies, like individuals, are part of an interconnected ecosystem.[48] They cannot ignore their suppliers' reality even though they are being well served. What happens within their ecosystem also matters, i.e. the companies' relationships with their direct suppliers and their suppliers' relationships with their suppliers. As a result of the tsunami, a new understanding of business relationships gained ground – they are broader, more holistic and far more complex than originally thought.

Other examples illustrate the impact of suppliers' decisions on companies. On Wednesday, April 24, 2013, when a building with over 3,000 people inside collapsed in Bangladesh, more than 1,000 people died. On Tuesday of that week, the facility had developed cracks in its façade. Local government officials visited the site and, according to some sources, suggested it be sealed up. The different businesses in the building included a garment manufacturer, a bank and some shops, but only the garment manufacturers showed up at work that day. The rest were told by their management to keep away from the building. The garment manufacturer supplied a number of major brands, but it did not release the brand names. It did not matter. The entire retail sector was experiencing a crisis due to the building collapse. Less than one month after the event, several Western retailers, including H&M, C&A and Inditex, agreed to support a new safety plan to prevent situations like this from happening again. These three multinationals were already some of the most committed to safety prevention and child labor throughout the globe, and yet, they were not able to keep track of the conditions their suppliers offered to employees. After the event, they partnered with their competitors, even those that were not directly affected by the scandal, to ensure better work conditions along their value chains and send a reassuring message to their final customers. This example shows the interrelationships between players in an ecosystem; a crisis

---

48. In this chapter, by collaborative ecosystem we mean a strategic business relationship among targeted companies to build a joint business strategy and destiny to generate sustainable value.

suffered by a competitor may end up sweeping you along if you do not take the necessary measures.

The future value chain structural and leadership shift: Taking the ecosystem into account

The situations above reflect the new challenges that value chain leaders face as part of their daily work. To be ready for them, companies regularly restructure in order to adapt to the fast-changing world. We often observe that, organizations reallocate their people based on internal rationalization models. In these cases, companies look at their own structure and tend to forget about the value chain's entire ecosystem that is required to offer their products or services to customers. In other words, the organizational design ignores the ecosystems built with other companies to successfully deliver the final product. We therefore propose that the future organization and staffing due diligence and methodologies integrate the above-mentioned broader picture, taking into account the connections with and among partners, suppliers and customers. The ecosystem should be the backbone of the company's structure.

Since the development of the early multidivisional companies, we know that organizational design should follow the strategy development phase. At the beginning of the 20th century, General Motors pioneered the multidivisional structure, by organizing numerous smaller automobile companies under a holding company. Ten years later, it was composed of more than 30 companies. Contrary to Ford's trend, which offered just one car model, GM's founder believed that he would reach more consumers by offering a wider range of cars.[49] So the divisions kept their car models and GM's organizational structure was adapted to their needs. Thus, the divisional structure allowed every division to focus on a clearly differentiated segment of customers, with differentiated products.

Every organizational design or structure has its advantages and challenges. Today, it is very common to find organizational models, such as matrix,

---

49. Chandler, Alfred D., Jr. *Strategy and Structure: Chapters in the History of the American Industrial Enterprise*. Cambridge, MA: MIT Press, 1962/1998.

geographical, functional, coordination committees, etc. One very insightful model for designing an appropriate structure is Galbraith's Star Model.[50] The Star Model includes five categories on which a company should base its design choice: strategy, structure, process, rewards and people. It proposes that these five elements ideally should be consistent and coordinated. However, we believe that the evolution of the value chain challenges this method. Specifically, the following considerations create a need to look for an alternative approach:

1. Value is generated by the interaction between customers and suppliers. The customer-supplier relationship is the foundation of any business transaction. Thus, the company structure must be designed and oriented to create the maximum value out of this interaction.

2. Value is most often the outcome of a collaborative ecosystem, and not only the result of the sum of different supply processes. Therefore, a company constrained by only one organizational model, may well be less flexible and be missing opportunities to generate value. That is why an organization designed around a collaborative ecosystem may develop a "blended organizational" model.

3. The design of an ecosystem-targeted organization cannot forget to include an in-depth leadership competencies and skills development reflection. Rather than leveraging on the traditional and generic leadership competency models, leaders will be asked to model the "collaborative ecosystem leadership competencies."

The value chain shift: An organizational design methodology

The VC2020 research project has explored organizational design and leadership development best practices. In this chapter, we describe an organizational and leadership design approach that might help companies evolve towards the development of a collaborative ecosystem.

---

50. Galbraith, Jay R. *Designing Organizations: An Executive Guide to Strategy, Structure, and Process.* San Francisco: Jossey-Bass, 2002.

It is a five-step process that goes from changing the company focus (from internal to external) to identifying the successful organization and leadership structure (processes, jobs, organization chart, interdependent key performance indicators, etc.) to mapping the competencies required for a job and staffing the role with the right person.

Because most value in the ecosystem is created by the interaction between customers and suppliers, the five-shift methodology is anchored on three main drivers to set the direction:

1. Identify the strategic potential of the customer and supplier relationship.

2. Differentiate and govern the customer and supplier relationships to develop sustainable and profitable value.

3. Organize the company to focus leaders' efforts on this pivotal and value-generating relationship.

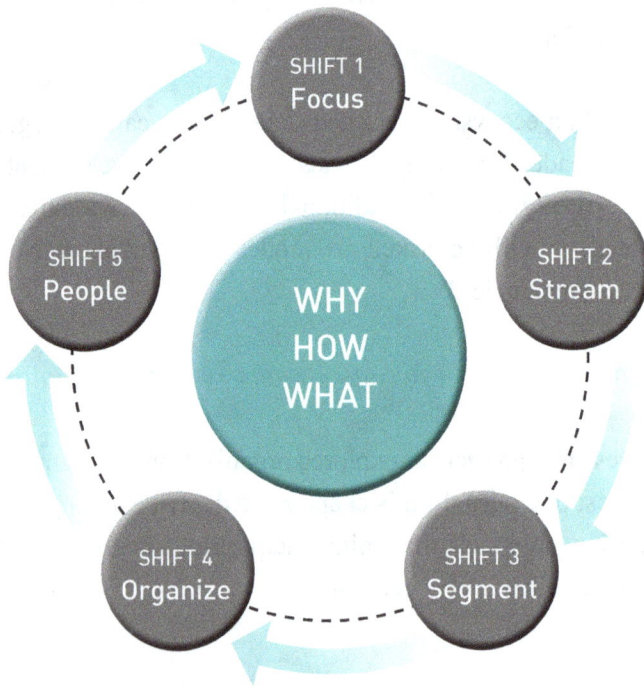

Figure 5.1: The five-shift methodology

As a result, the five-shift methodology has been developed (refer to *Figure 5.1*), articulated in five major steps to support the collaborative ecosystem organization design process:

1. Focus – from an in-house to a collaborative ecosystem focus.

2. Stream – from a broken to an integrated customer-supplier relationship.

3. Segment – from a diverse to a consistent segmentation.

4. Organize – from an internal to a collaborative ecosystem focus.

5. Develop people – from generic leadership to ecosystem leadership.

Shift 1: Focus – from an in-house to a collaborative ecosystem focus

This shift considers how to organize the customer-supplier relationship to better serve the overall value chain clients. Many organizations develop a strong in-house focus and in this configuration, suppliers are not connected with the company's customers. A collaborative ecosystem approach changes the relationships between the supplier, the organization, the customer and the end consumer. The ultimate goal of the organization's design is to serve not only its clients but to develop all parties along the value chain and foster a value generation culture. The objective is to unlock the value creation potential at any point where there is a selected and established connection.

The same scheme we apply to human relationships, which is based on interaction and the common benefit of all parts, should be applied to the new organizational model. The added value would then come from the synergies resulting from the company's relationship with all the key players in its value chain, from the first supplier to the end user. A sustainable relationship implies that the company works hand-in-hand with a group of selected players to succeed; and organize itself accordingly, that is all actors and even clients' clients who are connected to the organization's ecosystem, and they all have a specific role to play.

This shift requires a fundamental cultural change. The organization must ask itself, "Why not connect our suppliers with our customers if it can unlock a value generation opportunity?"

Companies with a traditional structure are oriented towards their clients and/ or suppliers only. The relationship from the supplier to the customer and the final client is linear. In the collaborative ecosystem organizational model that we studied, the relationship among parties is systemic and interconnected.

Shift 2: Stream – from a broken to an integrated customer-supplier relationship

Process integration and governance are critical for collaborative ecosystem development. The organizational bridge between sales and procurement is often broken. Most of the time, procurement focuses on reducing costs whereas sales focuses mainly on the top-line development.

We know that around 40% to 60% of innovation opportunities come from suppliers, who usually share and transfer them to the procurement organization – their only entry point. At the other end, clients are asking for innovation and they mainly interface with the organization through the sales department.

Both procurement and sales typically view the marketing and R&D departments as unique innovation drivers and miss opportunities to highlight the innovation coming from the company's suppliers. Therefore, suppliers' innovation proposals die before they reach the final customer. *Figure 5.2* depicts the barriers to collaboration that we often observe within in-house focused organizations. Specifically, the supplier interfaces with procurement whereas the end customer interacts with sales and marketing (S&M). The end customer requests innovation from S&M that the supplier would most likely be able to deliver if asked to do so. However, the two departments (S&M on the one hand and procurement on the other) work independently, blocking the communication and the innovation transfer. The innovation that the supplier could provide dies at procurement and never reaches the final customer.

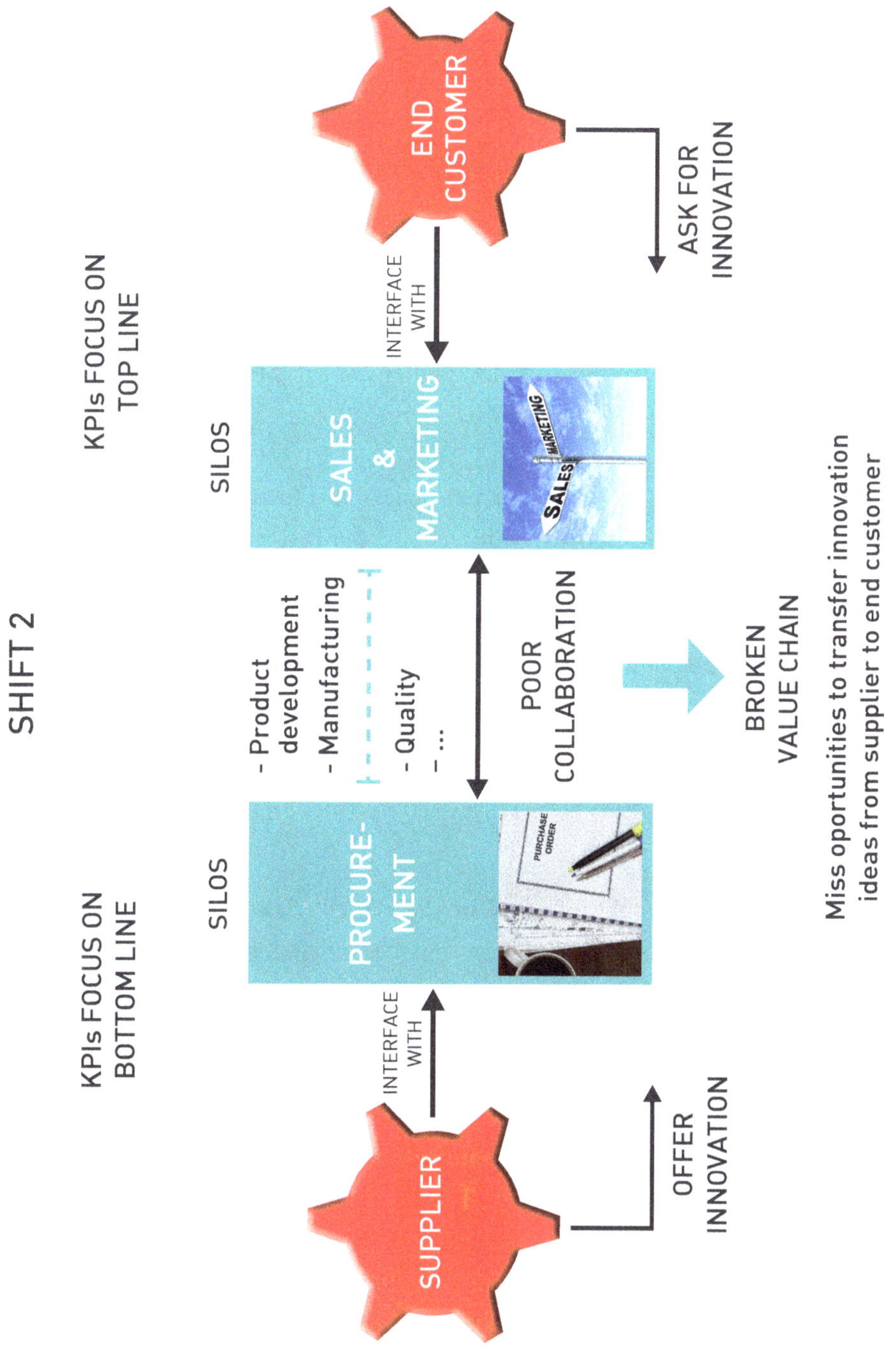

Figure 5.2: Shift 2 – stream[51]

51. Source: Emanuela Zappone, 2013. Photos: © Ragma Images, Lightspring –Shutterstock.com

Companies are missing opportunities to generate value by not leveraging the innovation that comes from suppliers. Shift 3 is the breakthrough that promotes information flow through the collaborative ecosystem.

Shift 3: Segment – from a diverse to a consistent segmentation

Often procurement and sales in companies use different models to segment their customers' and suppliers' portfolios. For example, procurement usually segments its suppliers based on how critical the commodities they provide are to the functioning of the company; whereas, sales mainly uses a financial approach, i.e. revenue per customer.

In this framework, even if procurement tries hard to leverage the innovation of its providers up through the value chain, the different segmentation used by the business units is a difficult obstacle to overcome because procurement does not really know where and how to leverage the supplier's innovation to answer to the company's customers' needs. The ecosystem information flow is blocked and the communication and knowledge transfer is broken and lost. Finding a common way to segment is a key prerequisite to breaking the gap between procurement and sales.

Professors Cordón and Vollmann defined the four stages of collaboration between customers and suppliers in their book *The Power of Two* (refer to *Figure 5.3*). Understanding how customers and suppliers interact is a prerequisite to differentiating and adapting the organizational design.

Based on their contribution, we propose the Collaborative Ecosystem Segmentation Framework – a two-by-two matrix that identifies innovation and process improvement as the two parameters for mapping the strategic potential of a customer-supplier relationship. This is the target collaboration along the collaboration stages defined by Professors Cordón and Vollmann and sets the foundation to open a differentiated organizational dialogue. *Figure 5.4* shows a real example of segmentation from the perspectives of both the customer and the supplier. The matrix on the left illustrates how customers, when asked to qualify their suppliers' ability to innovate or improve the customers' processes, positioned their suppliers in the matrix. The matrix on the right shows how suppliers

Strategic alignment	Senior management Strategic planning	Senior management Strategic planning
Value/cost	Design Procurement	Marketing Design
Total cost of ownership (TCO)	Accounting Industrial engineering Systems design	Accounting Industrial engineering Systems design
Flawless execution	Logistics Scheduling Manufacturing Quality	Sales Quality Manufacturing

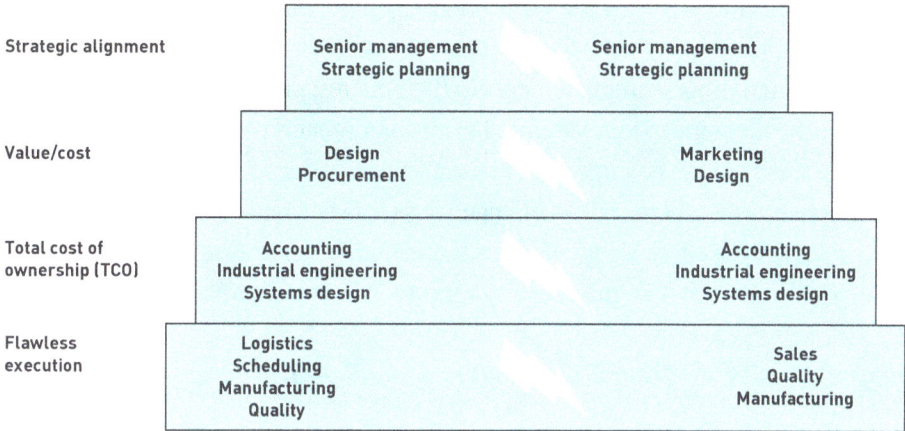

Figure 5.3: The four stages of collaboration[52]

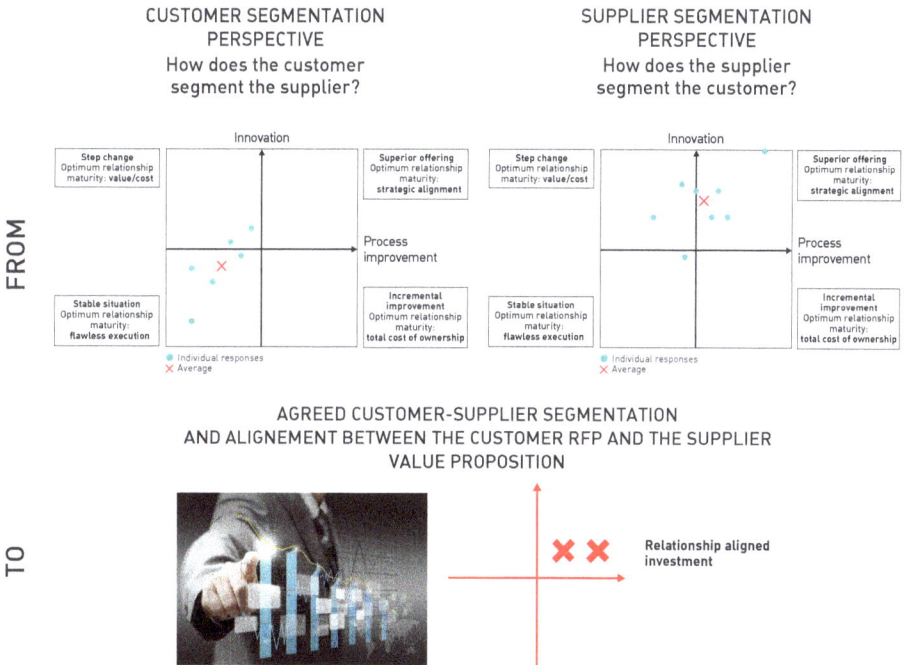

CUSTOMER SEGMENTATION PERSPECTIVE
How does the customer segment the supplier?

SUPPLIER SEGMENTATION PERSPECTIVE
How does the supplier segment the customer?

FROM

Innovation

Step change Optimum relationship maturity: value/cost	Superior offering Optimum relationship maturity: strategic alignment

Process improvement

Stable situation Optimum relationship maturity: flawless execution	Incremental improvement Optimum relationship maturity: total cost of ownership

● Individual responses
✕ Average

Innovation

Step change Optimum relationship maturity: value/cost	Superior offering Optimum relationship maturity: strategic alignment

Process improvement

Stable situation Optimum relationship maturity: flawless execution	Incremental improvement Optimum relationship maturity: total cost of ownership

● Individual responses
✕ Average

AGREED CUSTOMER-SUPPLIER SEGMENTATION
AND ALIGNEMENT BETWEEN THE CUSTOMER RFP AND THE SUPPLIER
VALUE PROPOSITION

TO

✕ ✕ Relationship aligned investment

Figure 5.4: Shift 3 – segment[53]

---

52. Cordón C. and T.E. Vollmann. *The Power of Two.* New York, NY: Palgrave Macmillan, 2008: 29.

53. Source: Emanuela Zappone, 2013. Photo: © Buchachon – Fotolia.com

101

answered the same question with regard to customers. As the graphic reflects, there is a misalignment in the perception suppliers and customers have of one another. Suppliers see themselves as more capable than their clients of offering innovation and process improvements to their clients; clients think their suppliers cannot offer them much innovation. This misalignment is partly because company business units tend to be immersed in their own dynamics without looking at their environment as a whole. The challenge we propose, as a first step to align their perceptions, is to agree on a common segmentation for customers and suppliers based on this two-by-two matrix (innovation × process improvement).

Shift 4: Organize – from an internal to a collaborative ecosystem focus

Each of the four collaboration stages defined in shift 3 of this process requires a specific organizational and people-oriented solution.

We suggest following the five-step path depicted in *Figure 5.1* to build a collaborative ecosystem-driven organizational design process. *Figure 5.5* shows the organizational focus changes required. *Activity mapping* focuses on obtaining a clear understanding of the objectives and activities required for the relationships in the ecosystem. *Process and governance mapping* compares the processes and governance structures of the relations and tries to understand them in order to create new joint processes. The *organization value model* supports the execution of the first two steps. *Job mapping* maps and redefines the jobs that the organization needs to serve its ecosystem and lastly, *staffing* will allocate the right talent to the right job.

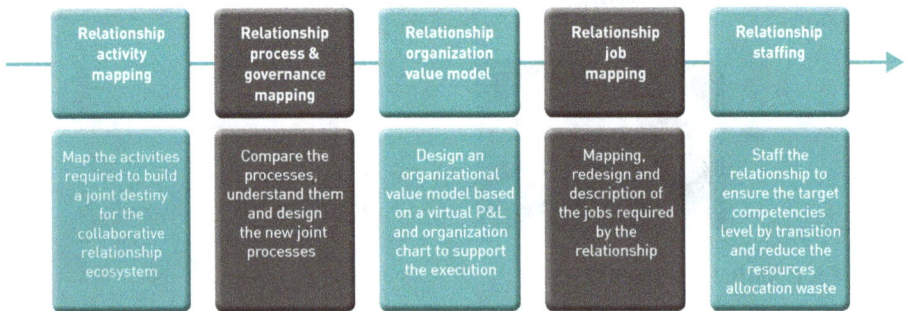

Relationship activity mapping	Relationship process & governance mapping	Relationship organization value model	Relationship job mapping	Relationship staffing
Map the activities required to build a joint destiny for the collaborative relationship ecosystem	Compare the processes, understand them and design the new joint processes	Design an organizational value model based on a virtual P&L and organization chart to support the execution	Mapping, redesign and description of the jobs required by the relationship	Staff the relationship to ensure the target competencies level by transition and reduce the resources allocation waste

Figure 5.5: Shift 4 – organize[54]

54. Source: Emanuela Zappone, 2013

As an outcome of the collaborative ecosystem organizational design process, the organizational strategy, as well as the jobs, the capabilities needed for each job, and the staffing criteria will be clear.

Shift 5: Develop people – from generic leadership to ecosystem leadership

Once the types of jobs have been defined and each position's capabilities identified, organizations try to answer the following questions:

- What are the competencies of the future?
- How do we identify good leaders?
- How do we develop that talent?

In the last step of shift 4, a company may realize that it is missing the type of talent the new organizational design requires. Shift 5 looks into this issue as well as the company's future to try to define the competencies that will be required.

Companies leverage the traditional leadership competencies models (e.g. generically by job function or job level) to assess their leaders. The proposed approach looks at competencies and behaviors across the collaborative ecosystem. Three leadership transitions characterize the customer-supplier relationship, i.e. the competencies required by leaders that administer, manage or sponsor the relationship.

Rather than looking at the level of the leader within the organization to define the level of expected leadership competencies, the focus is placed on the role that the employee plays in the customer-supplier relationship to determine the competencies that the employee needs to model. This includes bottom-level administrative positions up to top-level sponsors (refer to *Figure 5.6*).

Therefore, we mapped competencies required by the ecosystem for the following leadership transitions:

- Administrator transition: All competencies required by employees that make things work, i.e. they analyze and solve problems and execute effectively.

Collaborative ecosystem's relationship know-how

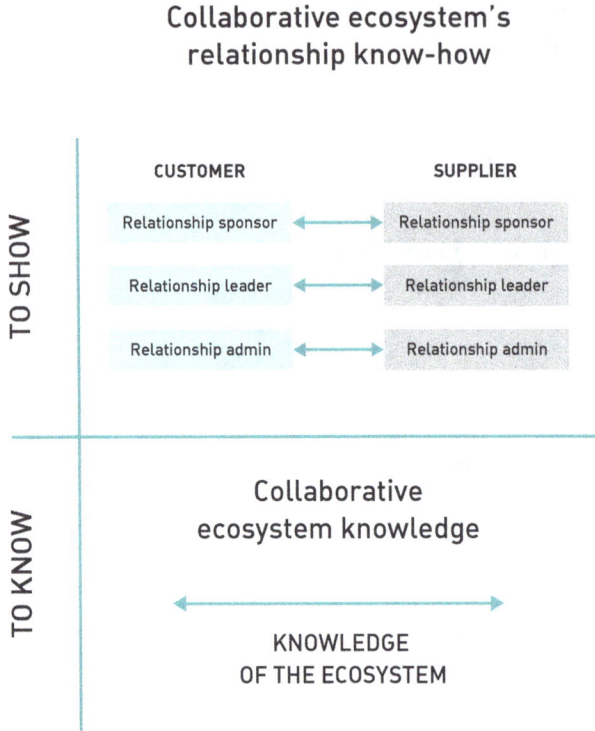

Figure 5.6: Shift 5 – develop people[55]

- Leader transition: All competencies required by leaders that drive the relationship. Tasks and competencies are based more on planning, identifying joint business opportunities and developing relationships than on execution.

- Sponsor transition: These leaders work at a very high level, sponsor the definition of a joint strategy, offer support to initiatives and projects that they believe in and foster collaboration across the ecosystem.

When looking at technical competencies classified as the "need-to-know" activities leaders need to effectively master their role (refer *to **Figure 5.6***), In the findings, we observed an on-going change: from a set of technical competencies oriented to specific business knowledge (by product, market,

---

55. Source: Emanuela Zappone, 2013.

company, etc.), to a set of technical competencies oriented to the deep knowledge of the collaborative ecosystem mechanisms.

Analyzing the organization along these five shifts will help determine the type of value chain leader that an organization needs in each role. Obviously, future value chain leaders will need some generic capabilities to succeed in 2020. The ability to see the broader picture and deal with complexity and cultural differences are some of them. Future leaders will work in a more collaborative and consultative environment, as part of a convergent world.[56] They will have to face new challenges that are difficult to foresee.

In the past, companies used to seek similar capabilities for all their purchasing or sales people, without looking at the role they played in the organization. In the future, sourcing and sales executives will need different capabilities depending on where their suppliers or customers are placed in the organization's ecosystem and the type of relationship between them, which will be defined by the type of segmentation used.

Managing will no longer be about dealing with commodities, but about dealing with and orchestrating different suppliers (who may supply several different commodities) or even networks of suppliers working together for the customer.

Key takeaways

- Companies are part of an ecosystem that includes suppliers, partners and customers. What affects the players in the ecosystem, will affect the company. A shift is needed to adapt organizations from a still predominant internal focus to a collaborative ecosystem orientation.

- Evolving from an internally focused model into an ecosystem requires an understanding of the company, its resources and its relationships with the ecosystem. The VC2020 research presents a new organizational design methodology to help companies succeed as they go through this transition.

---

56. Bulloch, Gib, Peter Lacy, and Chris Jurgens. "Convergence Economy: Rethinking International Development in a Converging World." *Accenture*, 2011.

The approach is to create a framework where leaders can focus more on relations with the external stakeholders rather than just internal stakeholders and customers.

- In a convergent world, the future value chain leaders will be exposed to new challenges that will require many capabilities to succeed. They are going to be leading teams of people from different companies rather than teams of internal people.

- When it comes to leadership transitions, managing relationships between customers and suppliers are more difficult than internal employee relationships. For the leader, it means unlearning past behaviors and learning to manage relationships with each player in the ecosystem.

Chapter 6
How speed affects risks, opportunities and new business models in value chains

Carlos Cordón

Chapter 6
How speed affects risks, opportunities and new business models in value chains

Carlos Cordón

Executive summary

The impact of speed on risks and opportunities is tremendous. While higher speed increases costs, it can also reduce risks and increase business opportunities. However, the "faster is better" maxim has its limitations. Depending on the industry and the context in which companies are operating, they need to determine their optimal speed.

Despite the fact that many companies would like to increase their speed because of the volatile context of recent years, increasing levels of control, bureaucracy and compliance regulations are decreasing speed and making companies more vulnerable to risks and less able to take advantage of opportunities.

The VC2020 research proposes a new model in this chapter that shows how companies can substantially improve both their speed and costs by standardizing products and removing variability. However, they need to find the right balance among speed, efficiency and variability. A supply chain or a process might be strong on two of these dimensions, but it cannot be strong on all three. The right speed falls at the point where the cost is minimized.

Clearly, it is in the best interests of companies to determine their optimal speed and manage it proactively. If they do not, their optimal speed may become irrelevant if the external environment changes abruptly. The challenge is that for many industries, speed is very much hardwired into their business models and the business models of the entire value chain. Therefore, changing speeds requires a business transformation for all the companies in the chain.

How speed affects risks, opportunities and new business models in the value chain

Introduction

March 2013 was the coldest in decades for much of Europe and the eastern United States.[57] The previous year another form of extreme weather had hit the US, heat waves, which many dubbed "March madness." The capriciousness of March weather spelled trouble for many fashion retailers. Hennes & Mauritz (H&M), the Swedish apparel giant, reported lower like-for-like sales in Q1 2013[58] attributing these disappointing results to unfavorable weather. Similarly, many fashion retailers in Europe experienced weak sales as a result of the relentlessly cold weather.

In contrast, Inditex, the world's biggest apparel company, reported an increase in sales during the same period. Inditex has a two-week cycle (from product design to delivery in its stores) while its competitors need months. If the weather is cold, Inditex delays the introduction of spring and summer clothing; if the weather is warmer, it promptly supplies spring clothing to its stores. This faster and more flexible supply chain allows the company to better manage weather risks and seize opportunities by adapting to short-term consumer trends. Inditex is credited with creating a new business model, fast-fashion, in which a fast supply chain is the critical element for success.

Is faster always better?

In the last two decades, a plethora of authors has praised the virtues of speed. Books like *Clockspeed* and *Time-based Competition* became classics in business management literature. Mostly, they claimed that faster was better. But even though we have become used to "internet speed" and "immediate consumption" many things are slower today than before (just think about the

---

57. In Germany, 2013 brought about the second coldest March in 50 years, while March 2012 was the country's third warmest on record. Source: Grieser, J. "Freezing cold March sets records across Europe." *Washington Post* blogs, Capital Weather Gang, March 29, 2013.

58. Milne R. "Late spring chills H&M sales." *Financial Times*, March 21, 2013.

time needed today to get a contract approval by internal legal departments or about the ever-increasing length of new drug approval processes).

If faster is always better, why does Inditex have a two-week cycle rather than, say, a one-day cycle? Clearly, the faster is better maxim is not without limitations. While higher speed generally creates potential opportunities, it comes at a cost. The right question to pose then is: what is the right speed?

Let us review two examples that shed light in the way companies in the pharmaceutical industry are dealing with this dilemma. The pharmaceutical industry is considered a low-speed industry with the typical manufacturer carrying 7 months of inventory. The entire value chain, down to the patient, holds about 9–10 months of inventory – triple or quadruple the inventories of many consumer goods segments.

In some exceptional cases, very high speeds are required. For example, in the case of a pandemic, vast quantities of flu vaccine have to be supplied within a very short time period to enable mass immunization of the population. Therefore, many manufacturers have built a lot of extra manufacturing capacity to be able to respond in the event of a pandemic. Because this capacity is idle most of the time, it represents a very high fixed cost, but it ensures high reaction speed. In this specific example, high speed reduces the risk of vaccine shortages, and in the event of a pandemic, it allows pharmaceutical companies to seize a huge business opportunity.

In the past, sales of many drugs used to have a relatively stable demand. Once patients were prescribed one drug, they would typically stay with the same drug for long periods of time. This stable demand did not require particularly fast speed, as changes in demand were very slow and the whole supply chain could be planned a long time in advance. By contrast, today, more and more health care players are becoming increasingly cost conscious. Some hold annual auctions for the supply of drugs and award contracts based on price. The company that wins the auction will have a sudden increase in demand; those that lose will have an abrupt drop in sales. Many traditional pharmaceutical companies are ill equipped to manage these sudden changes in demand. Further, some companies have such a slow reaction speed that they are not even able to respond to auction requests, which results in a substantial loss of business. In this example, the lack of speed means losing business opportunities. Higher speed has higher costs, reduces risks, increases business opportunities and might require companies to adopt a new business model.

Speed, risk, opportunities and the business model – theoretical frameworks

To better understand the interactions between speed, risk, opportunity and the business model, we looked at a few different frameworks to help clarify how those interactions might work.

First, we considered the concept of industry "clock speed" introduced by Charles Fine in the late 1990s.[59] For example, the aircraft industry has a low clock speed compared with the mobile phone industry, which has a high clock speed. The Boeing 747 is still in production, over 40 years after it was first launched, while a new model of the iPhone is launched every year or two. There are three clock speeds: product, process and the organizational clock speed, with the first being the fastest and the last the slowest. The challenge is that clock speeds become the set "way of doing things" in a company and changing them requires a business transformation.

Second, Marshall Fisher, who proposed that different products and services require different supply chains (see ***Figure 6.1***), argued that relatively standardized products and services (which he calls functional) necessitate supply chains that are efficient. As competition is predominantly price driven, it is understandable that companies pursue low-cost strategies in the supply chain. In contrast, the supply chains for differentiated products and services must be responsive to market demands to avoid obsolescence and losing business opportunities.

---

59. Fine, Charles H. Clockspeed: *Winning Industry Control in the Age of Temporary Advantage.* Reading, MA: Perseus Books, 1998.

	Efficient supply chain	Agile supply chain
Differentiated product/service	**Mismatch**	**Match**
Functional product/service	**Match**	**Mismatch**

Figure 6.1: Linking product and service characteristics to supply chain choice[60]

Finally, we propose a more comprehensive model by incorporating how the product variety and complexity influences the supply chain efficiency and speed. This requires including the effect of operational excellence projects. It is well documented that initiatives such as "lean" increase both speed and efficiency. One of the main drivers to obtain these benefits is to standardize products and remove variability. This reduction substantially improves both speed and costs. By contrast, increasing variability negatively affects both speed and efficiency.

The model we propose suggests that there is a balance between speed, efficiency and variability. A supply chain or a process might be strong on two of these three dimensions but not on all three.

For example, in a fast-food restaurant, the menu variety is strictly limited, which allows high speed (this is why it is called fast food) and high efficiency. It is also well known that these restaurants use standard processes for different products as much as possible.

---

60. Adapted from Fisher's conceptual supply chain-product match/mismatch matrix in Fisher, M.L. "What is the right supply chain for your product?" *Harvard Business Review* 75 (2), 1997: 105–116.

By contrast, a luxury restaurant is going to have a high variety of products, high speed and low efficiency (i.e. in the use of the restaurant's resources – waiters). Typically, in expensive restaurants, the proportion of personnel with respect to customers is higher than in fast-food restaurants. The service offered in a luxury restaurant is no waiting in a queue to be served; instead, the waiters will be available for you when you require them.

A third option is the typical family restaurant on the corner. It offers a high variety of products and high efficiency, but often its speed is slow. You might find "Aunt Maria" in the kitchen cooking a huge variety of meals and her siblings serving the food and chatting with the customers. The proposition is variety and efficiency of the resources, but probably slow speed on delivery.

This model is depicted in *Figure 6.2* as a triangle in which a supply chain should choose its position.

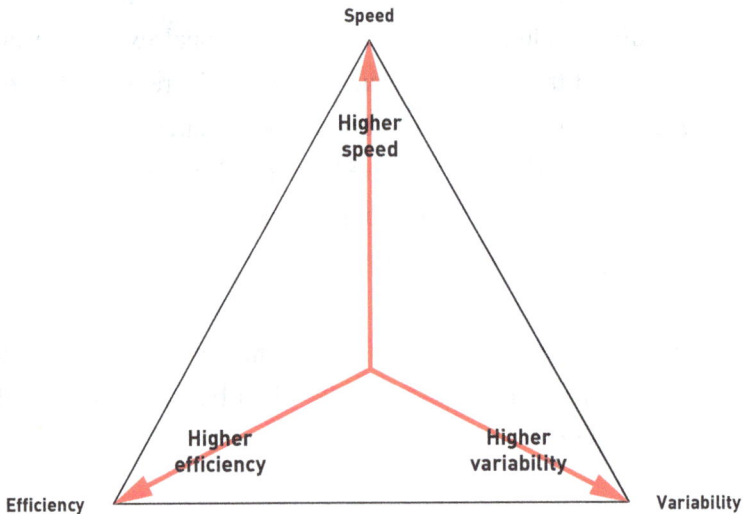

Figure 6.2: Balancing speed, efficiency and variability

It proposes that a business's supply chain occupies a position inside the triangle. It is not possible to be fast, efficient and highly variable at the same time. For example, a fast-food restaurant would be in the left part of the triangle – efficient and fast with low variability. A luxury restaurant would be in the right part – high speed and variety with low efficiency (thus, high cost).

If we compare this model with the agility and efficiency matrix in *Figure 6.1*, we see that a third dimension – variability – has been introduced. The matrix in *Figure 6.1* assumed that variety was higher in the agile supply chain and lower in the efficient supply chain.

In the pharmaceutical industry, companies try to diminish variability by promoting the exact same formulation for different countries, pushing variety to the last part of the supply chain – the packaging. This is called postponement and it is a way to increase speed and efficiency. One of the big challenges of personalized drugs is that the huge variety (a different product for every patient) required would make the supply chain either very expensive or very slow.[61]

While efficiency is easily measured by looking at costs, its impact on the bottom line is very easy to understand. However, the effect of speed and variety on company profit is not easy to quantify and understand. Thus, the impact of variety and speed are clear but not directly quantifiable. As a consequence, executives are forced to use their intuition to assess those effects.

Finding the right speed

Business leaders intuitively find an optimal speed and variety that maximizes profits while reducing risks and increasing the probability of taking advantage of opportunities. For example, two to three weeks is the right speed for Inditex to design a product and bring it to its stores. Traditional apparel businesses do this in six months on average, which sometimes results in products that consumers do not like or that are not suitable for the weather conditions (as we saw in our earlier example). Reducing this cycle further will be more expensive as it will require maintaining higher capacity levels. Either Inditex or its suppliers might need more equipment and/or more labor available to react at twice the speed.

---

61. Source: Miller, Henry I. "Personalized medicine may be good for patients but bad for drug companies' bottom line." *Forbes*, September 25, 2013. <www.forbes.com/sites/henrymiller/2013/09/25/personalized-medicine-may-be-good-for-patients-but-bad-for-drug-companies-bottom-line/> (accessed November 20, 2013).

Figure 6.3 depicts those trade-offs. The dotted line indicates the cost of operating at a given speed. The broken line indicates the expected cost of risk. This is equivalent to the probability of the risk happening (i.e. not having the right fashion products) multiplied by the damage incurred if the risk happens (i.e. sales lost for not having the right fashion products). The solid line represents the total cost obtained by adding both costs. The right speed is the point where the cost is minimized.

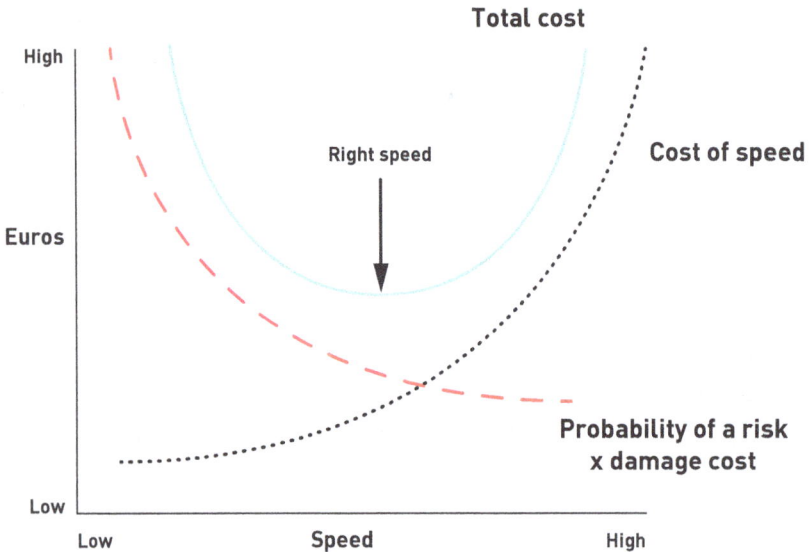

Figure 6.3: Trade-offs in optimizing speed

It should be emphasized that there are a many different types of risks and some of them are not influenced by speed. However, many of the ones related to supply chains, like the risk of obsolescence, risk of missing sales, damage caused by catastrophic risks (the faster the reaction the lower the damage) and quality risks (again, the faster the reaction the lower the damage), diminish with speed. These are the ones discussed in this chapter.

Institutionalization of speed: The company business model – a speed anchor or a speed burden?

As companies reach, what they believe, is the optimal speed, they institutionalize it and develop a business model that anchors that speed, i.e. forecasts are done weekly, management committee decisions are taken once a month, product development involves a certain number of steps which take, on average, three years, and so on.

When the external environment changes abruptly, however, organizations might find their speed is less than optimal. For example, in the aftermath of the 2008 financial and economic crisis, Philips' chief financial officer publically explained that the company was forced to trash its annual budget for 2009 and work with a three-month plan instead. The environment had become so volatile that the optimal speed for financial planning was higher, i.e. three months rather than one year.

Unfortunately, organizations tend to be anchored in certain speeds even though they no longer make sense. For example, today most organizations continue to pay their suppliers on a certain day of the month at 30-, 60- or 90-day intervals. Originally, that speed corresponded to the time it took to manually process invoices for payment. It also used to make sense to bring all of the paperwork to the bank at a given time of the month, instead of making constant trips. Though it is equally costly in today's Internet age to pay invoices at either 30-day or 15-day intervals, we continue with the "tradition" of paying every 30 days without questioning why.

In order to confront the established anchor and change the company speed, a transformation of the business model is often required. An example of speed being hardwired in the inner workings of a company can be found at an Asian company that was a traditional supplier trying to work with Inditex. When the company's executives, who were used to working with American companies, finally reached an agreement to sell lingerie products to Zara (owned by Inditex), they asked the Zara executives how long it would take Zara to process the purchase order. The answer stunned them. The buyer simply said, "I told you we are buying the product. If you want I can sign somewhere, but we must move quickly. There is no time for complicated processes; there is no process to approve orders." As a consequence, the supplier realized that before it could sell to Zara, it needed to transform its company. Its traditional six-month process was too slow. So it embarked on a three-year journey to reduce the process. After three years, it went back to Zara with a rapid new way of working. This time it was capable of meeting Zara's speed requirements.

The recent trend towards slower processes

The challenge in recent years is that many companies' and legal initiatives are decreasing speed and increasing the risks that they are supposed to diminish. In the area of purchasing, for example, a company in the aerospace industry realized that its purchase-to-pay process was composed of 132 steps. Similarly, while addressing the audience at a suppliers' day, the chief executive officer of a big multinational made a joke about the company not being capable of paying on time in spite of all its efforts. While both companies were trying to improve the relations and foster innovation with their suppliers, many of the suppliers felt that if the customer was not capable of paying on time, it meant its processes were out of control and, therefore, it would not have the capability to collaborate with them on innovation or process improvement.

The recent trend at Apple of spending more money on legal fights over patents than on innovation shows a total imbalance between resources and risks. Companies that spend so much time fighting over contracts for collaboration with external partners do not fully benefit from the joint development that could take place and, thus, lose business opportunities.

Finally, the compliance lawyers are becoming so obstructive in business that the risks that compliance rules are supposed to avoid are increasing dramatically due to the delays that result from the rules. It is becoming normal practice to sign contracts once the products are delivered because if this in not done, business stops. When business is conducted without contracts, the risks are greater.

Thus, while many companies would like to increase speed because of the volatile context of recent years, the increase in controls and compliance rules is reducing speed and, therefore, increasing risks and resulting in the current speeds being out of balance with the context in which companies are operating.

Key takeaways

- There is an optimal speed for any supply chain, process, company and industry. Faster is not always better; there is a cost to speed. The need for speed depends on the context; it is a balance between cost, opportunities and risks.

- Higher speed usually minimizes the effects of many risks and improves the probability of being able to take advantage of opportunities. Also, it is clear that higher speed, in general, comes at a higher cost.

- As the environment changes, what was considered the optimal speed, i.e. balancing cost with risk and opportunities, is not the best anymore. As uncertainty increases, there seems to be a clear need for more speed or more capacity.

- There is an optimal balance between speed, variability and cost. As a general rule, companies must chose to emphasize two of these dimensions at the expense of the other one.

- Organizations typically increase their levels of control and bureaucracy over time, which decreases speed and makes them more vulnerable to risks and less able to seize opportunities. This is particularly relevant in the value chain because it involves many different parts of the organization as well as many other organizations (suppliers, distributors, customers, etc.).

- Speed has a tremendous impact on risks and opportunities; therefore, it is imperative that organizations manage speed proactively. They should measure it and determine the optimum level for a given environment rather than react to events or demands.

Chapter 7

Corporate social responsibility: Moving from compliance to value creation in value chain relationships

Arjan van Weele
Luis Vivanco

Chapter 7

Corporate social responsibility: Moving from compliance to value creation in value chain relationships

Arjan van Weele
Luis Vivanco

Executive summary

Corporate social responsibility (CSR) is a relatively recent term, but as far back as the 1930s, some companies were already providing employees with housing and other benefits. CSR is about the relationship between the corporation and society, whereby a company's actions not only serve its shareholders' financial needs, but also benefit other stakeholders. This results in multiple implications for companies. At its broadest, societal expectations, which are influenced by and transmitted through NGOs, provide the operational framework for companies over and above traditional laws provided by governments. Companies that fail to see this do so at their peril and often pay dearly.

But a company's CSR efforts will ultimately fail if the actions it takes to benefit society are PR driven and ancillary to the company's strategy. It is only those companies that are able to incorporate CSR as a core component of their strategies and operations that will be able to turn it into a source of competitive advantage. For this to happen, the mindset of creating wealth (for the company) must change to creating value (for everyone). This requires an understanding of where CSR efforts can have the biggest impact across the whole value chain in relation to the company's position in it. Carbon footprint and supplier inclusion will be more important to upstream companies in the value chain, while product safety and environmental friendliness are more relevant to companies that are closer to the final consumer.

The rising importance of corporate social responsibility

The video starts like countless other commercials of its type. A young man bears the boredom of a routine job at the office, looking up now and then at the wall clock in a hopeless desire to see time pass. The screen breaks to a red background with familiar white type asking the question, "Are you ready for a break?" The young man takes out a Kit Kat and starts to open it revealing an ape finger in lieu of the chocolate bar. He nonchalantly takes the finger as his co-workers look on not knowing whether to warn him. He bites into the finger, and a small jet of blood drips down his chin and onto his computer's keyboard. Oblivious to it all, he wipes his mouth with the back of his hand, spreading blood all over his chin before the screen cuts to an orangutan and asks the viewers to demand that Nestlé (the maker of Kit Kat outside the US) stop buying palm oil from suppliers that destroy rainforests – the orangutan's habitat.

The video, made by Greenpeace, went viral on YouTube and, as a result, Nestlé announced a partnership with the Forest Trust to establish "responsible sourcing guidelines" to ensure that its products did not have a deforestation footprint. Nestlé also announced that it would work with all of its supply chain actors to ensure that by 2015, they were harvesting palm oil using fully sustainable methods.[62] The validity of Greenpeace's claim against Nestlé was, in fact, of little relevance, as it was being judged in the court of public opinion rather than in a court of law. The situation exposed how vulnerable Nestlé could be to events outside its traditional control, up or down the supply chain, due to the increasing weight that society was placing on corporate social responsibility.

Global trends

The advent of the Internet and social media has fostered the massive growth of NGOs. Since the mid-1990s, NGOs have emphasized humanitarian issues, development aid and sustainable development partly as a reaction to the

---

62. "Nestlé committed to traceable sustainable palm oil to ensure no-deforestation." *Nestlé*, October 30, 2012. <www.nestle.com/Media/Statements/Pages/Update-on-deforestation-and-palm-oil.aspx> (accessed September 11, 2013).

increase in globalization after the fall of the Soviet Union.[63] While they are not in a position to draft government policy or enact laws, NGOs have the ability to affect businesses by indirectly influencing governments to establish business regulations according to the interests they support, or directly by influencing consumer perceptions of given companies, as was the case with Greenpeace, which pushed Nestlé to react.

The concepts behind CSR are nothing new, and back in the 1930s, Dutch multinational Philips was already providing housing, education and health care for its employees. However, the discussion has moved in the past decades to defining the scope of these corporate responsibilities.

One of the problems with corporate social responsibility is that its very definition is so vague and intangible that it can mean anything to anyone, and therefore, it is effectively without meaning.

The prevailing view for most of the 20th century was that a business's only social responsibility was to maximize profits for its shareholders. The economist Milton Friedman opposed the idea of expanding this responsibility on the basis that it imposed an unfair and costly burden on the company and vis-à-vis competitors. However, this view is no longer considered acceptable and the concepts of the stakeholder theory championed by a number of economists and social scientists suggest that corporations are responsible not only to their shareholders but also to other stakeholders. These groups include customers, suppliers, employees, the societies where companies operate, consumer or environmental advocacy groups, etc. Corporations' new responsibilities include responding to the economic, legal, ethical and philanthropic expectations of their stakeholders. They must fulfill the expectation of creating shareholder value within the regulatory and legal framework in which they operate. While these two requirements have been traditional corporate obligations, companies also increasingly have to comply with ethical responsibilities and behaviors that are not necessarily codified into law but are expected by society, or they may even undertake voluntary philanthropic activities.

63. Zaleski, Pawel. "Global non-governmental administrative system: Geosociology of the third sector." In Gawin, Dariusz and Piotr Glinski (eds), *Civil Society in the Making*. Warszawa: IFiS Publishers, 2006.

CSR as an integral part of the organization

The orthodox view of profitability within the law as the sole motive of an organization (a view that was accepted up to the 1970s) places companies at peril and those that simply comply with existing laws can increasingly find themselves in situations like the one that Nestlé's Kit Kat cocoa sourcing triggered.

Drivers of CSR

Governments and multilateral institutions are no longer the drivers of corporate social responsibility change; instead, they often simply follow existing trends by creating legislation that formalizes them. The advent of social media has empowered small NGOs with limited financial resources that are able to strike the right idea. Corporate rankings in magazines have become points of reference for CEOs of most, if not all, multinationals.[64] In the past, society neither demanded that companies engage in CSR initiatives nor punished them for failing to do so; nowadays, however, companies must carefully consider the growing expectations placed on them in order to compete.

CSR has become a boardroom issue

CEOs of large multinationals are both the targets of NGOs and societal-driven pressure and the leaders of the changes taking place. CSR has become a boardroom issue with its strategy set as an integral part of the overall company strategy. In the past, companies would sponsor PR-related activities that had little or nothing to do with the business; today corporate sustainability is a strategic differentiator. The effects of this change in approach have been enormous. Large corporations are considered bigger promoters of global sustainability than consumers, NGOs or governments.[65]

---

64. "Six growing trends in corporate sustainability." *Ernst & Young*, 2013. <www.ey.com/US/en/ Services/Specialty-Services/Climate-Change-and-Sustainability-Services/Six-growing-trends-in-corporate-sustainability_overview> (accessed September 11, 2013).

65. "Six growing trends in corporate sustainability." *Ernst & Young*, 2013. <www.ey.com/US/en/ Services/Specialty-Services/Climate-Change-and-Sustainability-Services/Six-growing-trends-in-corporate-sustainability_overview> (accessed September 11, 2013).

CSR and value creation

Those corporations that create value, or are looking to create value through CSR do so with a triple profit line in mind: people (inside and outside the company), planet and profit.[66] The question is: how can these seemingly opposing goals be achieved? Based on a study of 30 large organizations,[67] it can be concluded that sustainability, when well ingrained, leads to organizational and technological innovations that have a positive impact on both revenues and profits. From an opportunistic standpoint, there are benefits to embracing sustainability as an integral part of a company's strategy:

- *Stage 1: Viewing compliance as an opportunity.* Being the first to adopt emerging laws allows companies more time to experiment with creative solutions and spot new business opportunities. It may also reduce costs as one single chain is required for all markets, rather than having to adapt it to the variations of each set of regulations.

- *Stage 2: Making value chains sustainable.* Once companies have learned to keep pace with regulation, they become more proactive about sustainability, particularly about environmental issues such as resource use. This initially helps the company's image, but down the line, it also helps reduce costs and create new businesses.

- *Stage 3: Designing sustainable products and services.* Improved supply chain management allows a company to take a closer look at its product structures, redesign them to meet customer concerns and examine the products' life cycles.

- *Stage 4: Developing new business.* New business models provide alternatives to the current way of doing business while succeeding in the value delivery to the customer. These often materialize in collaborations

---

66. Elkington, J. *Cannibals with Forks: The Triple Bottom Line of 21st Century Business.* Oxford: Capstone, 1997.

67. Nidumolu, R., C.K. Prahalad and M.R. Rangaswami. "Why sustainability is now the key driver of innovation." *Harvard Business Review*, Vol. 87, September 2009: 57–64.

with other companies like when FedEx integrated its chain with Kinko's so that documents could be printed on location rather than being shipped.

- *Stage 5: Creating next-practice platforms.* Corporations move from looking for ways to deliver value that are compatible with CSR and sustainability, to making sustainability the main tenet through which business models are created.

Figure 7.1 presents the challenges, required competencies and opportunities of each stage.[68]

Within this operating framework, sustainability is thus the key driver of innovation and far from yesterday's burden on financial performance that many executives took it to be. Furthermore, it can be said that it will become a prerequisite for attaining competitive advantage, but it will require an overhaul of existing business models, products, technologies and processes.

Implementing CSR

The lack of a consensus regarding what constitutes CSR leaves room for a wide variation in the implementation of CSR across different companies and industries. This is true throughout the plan-do-check-act cycle. There are commonalities about the issues companies touch on: people (employees, customers, communities), planet (carbon, water, waste), product (safety, materials), process (value chain, responsible business practices), but differences on the priority they give to each depending on their industry. *Figure 7.2* presents the plan-do-check-act cycle.

The divergent approaches may be a good thing, as each company is able to place their efforts where they can have the biggest positive impact. Problems may arise when the initiatives are PR driven and unrelated to the fundamental business model of the company. This will foster a CSR strategy that is dependent on a CSR department with a limited budget, rather than one that is intertwined with the company's strategy.[69]

---

68. Nidumolu, R., C.K. Prahalad and M.R. Rangaswami. "Why sustainability is now the key driver of innovation." *Harvard Business Review*, Vol. 87, September 2009: 57–64.

69. VC2020 research.

STAGE 1 Viewing Compliance as Opportunity	STAGE 2 Making Value Chains Sustainable	STAGE 3 Designing Sustainable Products and Services	STAGE 4 Developing New Business Models	STAGE 5 Creating Next-Practice Platforms
CENTRAL CHALLENGE To ensure that compliance with norms becomes an opportunity for innovation.	**CENTRAL CHALLENGE** To increase efficiences throughout the value chain.	**CENTRAL CHALLENGE** To develop sustainable offerings or redesign existing ones to become eco-friendly.	**CENTRAL CHALLENGE** To find novel ways of delivering and capturing value, which will change the basis of competition.	**CENTRAL CHALLENGE** To question through the sustainability lens the dominant logic behind business today.
COMPETENCIES NEEDED >>The ability to anticipate and shape regulations. >>The skill to work with other companies, including rivals, to implement creative solutions.	**COMPETENCIES NEEDED** >>Expertise in techniques such as carbon management and life-cycle assessment. >>The ability to redesign operations to use less energy and water, produce fewer emissions, amd generate less waste. >>The capacity to ensure that suppliers and retailers make their operations eco-friendly.	**COMPETENCIES NEEDED** >>The skills to know which products or services are most unfriendly to the environment. >>The ability to generate real public support for sustainable offerings and not be considered as "greenwashing". >>The management know-how to scale both supplies of green materials and the manufacture of products.	**COMPETENCIES NEEDED** >>The capacity to understand what consumers want and to figure out different ways to meet those demands. >>The ability to understand how partners can enhance the value of offerings.	**COMPETENCIES REQUIRED** >>Knowledge of how renewable and nonrenewable resources affect business ecosystems and industries. >>The expertise to synthesize business models, technologies, and regulations in different industries.
INNOVATION OPPORTUNITY >>Using compliance to induce the company and its partners to experiment with sustainable technologies, materials, and processes.	**INNOVATION OPPORTUNITIES** >>Developing sustainable sources of raw materials and components. >>Increasing the use of clean energy sources such as wind and solar power. >>Finding innovative uses for returned products.	**INNOVATION OPPORTUNITIES** >>Applying techniques such as biomimicry in product development. >>Developing compact and eco-friendly packaging.	**INNOVATION OPPORTUNITIES** >>Developing new delivery technologies that change value-chain relationships in significant ways. >>Creating monetization models that relate to services rather than products. >>Devising business models that combine digital and physical infrastructures.	**INNOVATION OPPORTUNITIES** >>Building business platforms that will enable customers and suppliers to manage energy in radically different ways. >>Developing products that won't need water in categories traditionally associated with it, such as cleaning products. >>Designing technologies that will allow industries to use the energy produced as a by-product.

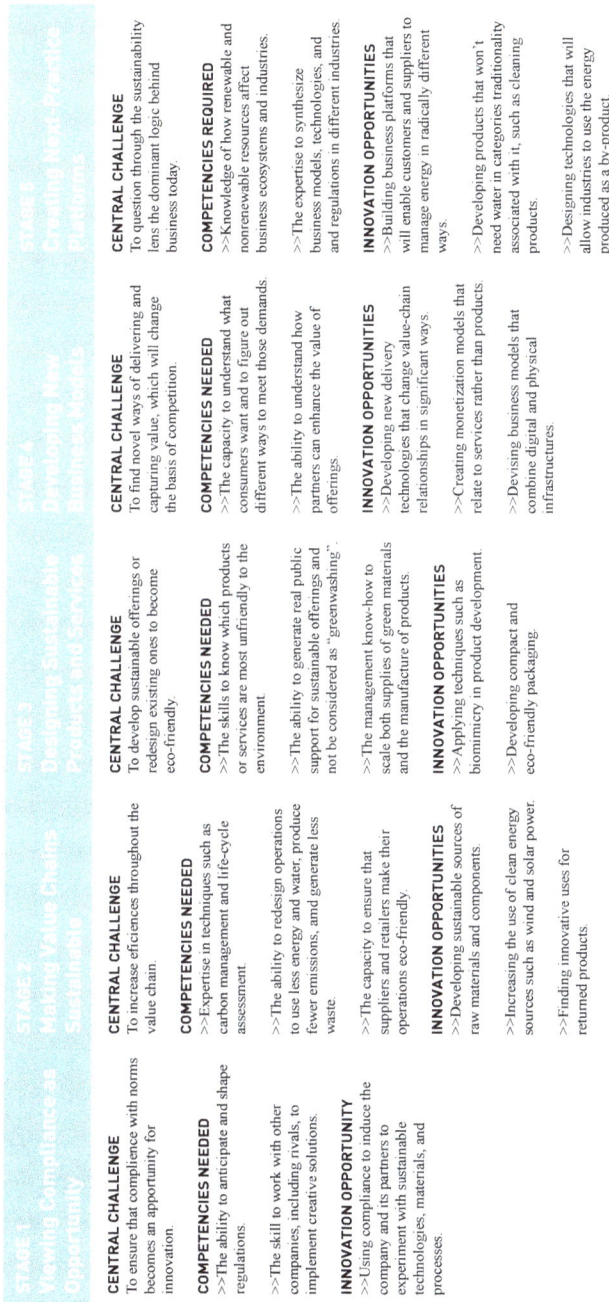

Figure 7.1: Stages in the adoption of CSR by organizations[70]

---

70. Nidumolu, R., C.K. Prahalad and M.R. Rangaswami. "Why sustainability is now the key driver of innovation." *Harvard Business Review*, Vol. 87, September 2009: 57–64. (Figure 7.1 is reproduced with permission.)

Figure 7.2: Plan-do-check-act cycle[71]

Plan

Companies must have ambitious, long-term goals, corresponding budgets, organization-wide integration efforts and thorough employee involvement. The governance structure should extend to the board level, while at the operational level, each business unit should have sustainability councils and measurements in place.

Do

In a nutshell, CSR is about the relationship between the corporation and society and any related action by the company must be done in partnership with a valid representative of society (for each specific issue that is addressed). The external partner may be an NGO (such as the Forest Trust and Nestlé or Nigeria Dental Association and Unilever) a private institution, policymakers or research institutes.

71. Source: Porter, Michael E. and Mark T. Kramer. "Creating shared value: How to reinvent capitalism and unleash a wave of innovation and growth." *Harvard Business Review*, January/February, 2011: 62–77. (Figure 7.2 is reproduced with permission.)

Check

A CSR initiative must not only deliver value to the society it is supposed to serve but also measure that value in a way that is both objective and independent. Companies know this and, as a result, they have made great progress towards being transparent through a wide range of instruments that include internal and external audits, codes of conduct for employees and suppliers, links to sustainability indexes, etc.

Act

Although ambitions are high and initiatives numerous, most companies seem to lack a systematic method for analyzing the actual business benefits obtained through their CSR programs. Their initiatives do not seem to be tailored to specific programs, and the results they deliver, at both the corporate and particularly the business-unit level, are not compared with initial targets. This failure to compare becomes an impediment to organizational learning. Stakeholders, both internal and external, must participate, including at the local level.

CSR and the value chain

Many companies have redesigned their business models in a way that they retain relatively few core activities and outsource the rest. This increases their dependence on suppliers and makes their procurement and supply chain management functions more important. Large corporations can influence the CSR policies of their suppliers through codes of conduct. In turn, just as it does internally, the new standards can foster the suppliers' innovation, which will result in a direct benefit for the company, its customers and society.[72]

A company can only preach what it practices, and it must establish a CSR policy before attempting to engage suppliers. Once this is done, the impact can be enormous. In a company like Unilever, its manufacturing processes account for 3% to 4% of its products' total carbon footprint, while 26% comes from the

---

72. Kibbeling, M.I. "Creating value in supply chains: Supplier's impact on the value for customers, society and shareholders." PhD Dissertation, *Technische Universiteit Eindhoven*, 2010.

activities upstream, i.e. from the extraction and procurement of raw material to the products it acquires from its suppliers. Furthermore, if it worked with its suppliers, it could lead to better packaging and other product improvements that would reduce the footprint at the consumer level.

Driving CSR in the supply chain

What do large companies do to drive CSR in their supply chain relationships? What programs do they have in place? And what actions are most effective? As CSR is still a relatively new and developing concept in many companies, these questions are not easy to answer. Nonetheless, the efforts by some large international companies offer some worthy examples.

The first and most encouraging observation is that almost all major companies today have CSR integrated into their mission statement and business strategies. However, the degree to which they attempt to project CSR to their suppliers varies widely. At the operational level, CSR initiatives seem to be sector specific and highly correlated with their relative position in the value chain. Companies that operate downstream in their value chains, i.e. consumer goods manufacturers (Unilever and Nestlé, but also companies like Lego and Philips) and retailers (like Ikea and Walmart), seem to emphasize product safety and environmental friendliness in their stakeholder relationships. Their prime concern is safeguarding their brand image and reputation. Companies operating upstream in the value chain, closer to the raw materials than to the consumer (Shell, DSM and AKZO Nobel) stress the importance of carbon footprint reduction, compliance and worker safety both internally and in their relationships with suppliers and sub-contractors.

Most large companies today have specific supplier sustainability codes of conduct in place, which suppliers are expected to sign and the company then follows up on them. Follow-up is especially important with low-cost country suppliers, as experience indicates that while many sign the code of conduct, it is not reflected in their operations. These companies adopt existing standards and norms, rather than creating new ones, which result in a consistent measurement rationale.

Companies sometimes engage in activities aimed at improving supplier sustainability. Nestlé, Unilever, Mars and FrieslandCampina, among others, have invested heavily in programs aimed at helping local farmers in developing countries improve their product quality, operational efficiency and crop productivity. Sometimes their focus is more specific and aimed at promoting businesses owned by ethnical minorities and/or women.

Any initiative must use the right key performance indicators (KPIs) to ensure that it is meeting its objectives. At the most basic level: the percentage of expenditure that is sourced sustainably, the number of supplier sustainability audits conducted and the percentage of suppliers that have signed the supplier code of conduct. Beyond these, measures may reflect actual carbon emission reduction in the supply chain, the number of casualties/injuries of workers and the number of supplier code violations. Yet, further discussion is required on if and how sustainability KPIs should be part of the procurement professional's personal dashboard and bonus system. A conscious assessment needs to be made of how much responsibility a company should assume in driving CSR principles in its second- and third-tier supplier relationships. *Table 7.1* provides an overview of the concepts and tools used by companies to drive CSR in their supply chain relationships.

Creating shared value

The irony of corporate social responsibility is the more a company embraces it and the more transparent it becomes, the more society blames the company for its failures. Governments react by setting policies that undermine companies' competitiveness resulting in companies being caught in a vicious cycle. So while CSR as a general approach, and sustainability in particular, can be beneficial to the long-term strategy of a company, the initiatives fail to extract all the potential advantages as they concentrate on reputation and are only obliquely related to the business. This makes it hard to justify the policies in hard times and over the long term. Creating shared value (CSV) seems like a better guideline for companies when making investment decisions in a community, as CSV is an integral part of a company's profitability and competitive position[73] (see *Table 7.2*).

---

73. Porter, Michael E. and Mark T. Kramer. "Creating shared value: How to reinvent capitalism and unleash a wave of innovation and growth." *Harvard Business Review*, January/February, 2011: 62–77.

Stakeholder management	Supply chain sustainability strategy	Supplier relationships	Competence development	External standards	Supply chain sustainability measures
•Stakeholder meetings on creating shared value (in water, nutrition, rural development, energy, environmental stewardship) •Expert opinion panels for leadership •Corporate social responsibility committee •Sustainability part of vision and mission statements •Corporate citizenship	•Value chain carbon neutral/carbon emission reduction •Support local buying in countries where sales are made •Water management plan across supply chain •Farmer productivity programs •Secure long-term raw material availability •Product life cycle approach •Increase share of renewable energy •Supplier sustainability involvement program •Supplier HS&E programs •Fuel efficiency program •Business travel program	•Supplier quality assurance •Responsible sourcing traceability program •Supplier compliance to local legal requirements •Supplier sustainability audits •internal •external •Supplier sustainability self assessment •Supplier sustainability improvement plan •Code of business ethics •Supplier code of conduct responsible sourcing guidelines •Identification of critical suppliers •Supplier sustainability risk profile •On-line responsible procurement system •Contractual commitment •Supplier diversity program •Human rights impact assessment	•Training buyers in responsible procurement practices •E-learning course on responsible procurement practices •Training buyers in supplier quality assurance •Employee engagement •Supplier training and competency building •Supplier development programs •Citizenship program for employees	•Global Reporting Initiative/G3 •UN CEO Water Mandate •Dow Jones Sustainability Index •Pharmaceutical Security Institute •NGO Fair Labor Association •ISO 14001 •EICC Code of Conduct •FTSE4GOOD •FSC •Carbon Disclosure Leadership Index (CDLI)	•Supply chain carbon dashboard/carbon emissions •% sustainable suppliers •% sustainable purchasing spend •Globe scan reputation survey •Employee engagement index •Supplier compliance rates •Supplier working hours •Supplier code of conduct violations

Table 7.1: Concepts and tools used to drive CSR in supply chain relationships[74]

With a CSV proposition, people and planet are no longer contingent on the main objective of profit but become resources and enablers of this profit. The difference between CSR and CSV is that the former looks at creating wealth (for the company), part of which is then given back to the community, while the latter aims to jointly create value (for all). Adapting the principle of shared value implies a redefinition of the purpose of a company from profit maximization to creating shared value as Porter and Kramer show in the next table.

A CSR approach may look, for example, at fair trade initiatives that enlarge the share of revenues or profits of a selected set of suppliers through

---

74. VC2020 research.

CSR	CSV
Value: Doing good	Value: Economic and societal benefits relative to cost
Citizenship, philanthropy, sustainability	Joint company and community value creation
Discretionary or in response to external pressure	Integral to competing
Separate from profit maximization	Integral to profit maximization
Agenda is determined by external reporting and personal preferences	Agenda is company specific and internally generated
Impact limited by corporate footprint and CSR budget	Realign the entire company budget
Example: Fair trade purchasing	Example: Transforming procurement to increase quality and yield.

Table 7.2: From corporate social responsibility to creating shared value[75]

redistribution; a supplier's gain is another supplier's loss. CSV looks at how improvements in the value chain can be jointly achieved to expand the overall value created in a way that all stakeholders benefit. Value creation needs to be defined not in terms of benefits by themselves, but in terms of how they relate to costs. Shared value requires companies to include externalities or social costs (such as pollution) in their measure of performance. Finally, a CSV-focused strategy will incur higher initial investments, but the economic and societal benefits will be greater for all stakeholders.

Conclusion

CSR is, in many ways, still in its infancy. Most companies are aware of its importance but they are yet to define how best to incorporate it in their strategies. As a result CSR initiatives, of which there is a broad portfolio, suffer from a lack of focus and measurement tools to determine their effectiveness. In part, this is due to CSR being conducted as an activity separate from the company's business, under a separate CSR department's budget and discretion, rather than as a function that is intertwined with the business practices.

---

75. Porter, Michael E. and Mark T. Kramer. "Creating shared value: How to reinvent capitalism and unleash a wave of innovation and growth." *Harvard Business Review*, January/February, 2011: 62–77.

- If CSR is going to be an integral part of the business, as it should be, sustainability practices must be linked to performance targets, just like other business practices, and they must have a demonstrable impact on the business.

- The most profitable initiatives for the company should be those that achieve a wide set of targets that include both direct economic and societal benefits. Where a company sits in the value chain largely determines the type of CSR efforts that it will initiate, be they aimed at the consumer, suppliers, employees and/or the society. A company's CSR activities must be a balanced mix of internal (process and employee-related sustainability initiatives) and external (supplier- and community-related) initiatives.

- Finally, the alignment of company, suppliers, communities and consumers can only be reached if the company's approach is to create value, rather than redistribute wealth. Furthermore, this will assist corporations in addressing the expectations that societies are placing on them.

Key takeaways

- Companies' behavior is increasingly being dictated by societal expectations. The ability to react to chang eaningful impact, players up and down the value chain must be engaged in carbon footprint reducing initiatives.

- CSR themes seem to be different depending on where a company resides in the value chain. The more upstream, the more the company will focus on compliance and carbon dioxide reduction, while those companies that are more downstream (closer to the end consumer/user), the more they will occupy themselves with social value and brand reputation.

- In driving sustainability, companies place a lot of importance on audits and compliance with rules and guidelines when dealing with suppliers. Less attention is paid to what is in it for the suppliers to comply and to understand the effects of this top-down approach on supplier operations and innovativeness.

- A company's ability to reduce its footprint is often limited by its boundaries in the value chain. To have a meaningful impact, players up and down the value chain must be engaged in carbon footprint reducing initiatives.

www.ingramcontent.com/pod-product-compliance
Lightning Source LLC
Chambersburg PA
CBHW061332220326
41599CB00026B/5141